TODAY'S CATHOLIC

TODAY'S CATHOLIC

EDMUND FLOOD, O.S.B.

Darton Longman and Todd
London

First published in Great Britain in 1980
Darton, Longman & Todd Ltd
89 Lillie Road
London SW6 1UD

ISBN 0 232 51473 9

Printed in Great Britain by
Richard Clay (The Chaucer Press) Ltd
Bungay, Suffolk

Practical Theology Series

Editors' Introduction

The Vatican Council ended in 1965. It ratified for the whole Catholic Church a policy of living the Christian life in closer touch with the perspectives of the Bible: love more than law, community more than hierarchy, affirmation of the world more than distrust, the unique worth of the individual more than uniformity.

The Catholic Church has now had fifteen years of experience of these principles: of the hope they bring, the problems and opportunities of implementing them, and above all our need of them as we face the challenges of the future.

Written for the ordinary Catholic, this series describes where we have got to. It recalls that magnificent view of God's relationship with his People in the world of today and what we have so far done about establishing the Kingdom. It tries to see the implications of all this for the decisions we have to make today as individual Catholics who are members of the Church.

Edmund Flood, O.S.B.
John Coventry, S.J.

Today's Catholic is the introductory volume to the **Practical Theology Series**.

CONTENTS

	Acknowledgements	viii
	Preface	ix
1	The End of a Long Winter?	1
2	Invitation Towards Summer	3
3	Family Life	9
4	The Church and Divorce	22
5	Prayer	33
6	Christian Leadership	51
7	Today's Catholic	82
8	And Now?	106
	Notes	112
	Further Reading	116

ACKNOWLEDGEMENTS

The author would like to express his thanks to the publishers of *The Tablet* for permission to reproduce extracts from previously published work.

Biblical quotations are taken from the Jerusalem Bible, published and © 1966, 1967 and 1968 by Darton, Longman & Todd Ltd. and Doubleday & Co. Inc., and are used by the permission of the publishers.

PREFACE

The Vatican Council finished in 1965. It gave every member of the Church an opportunity to capture a fuller kind of Christian life.

It takes time to absorb new perspectives. These were not merely unfamiliar but also challenging. The Council stressed our responsibilities to the world. We needed to reflect and experiment.

How is the Council's much richer—because more biblical—understanding of Christianity affecting the life of today's Catholic? Each Catholic asks that with regard to his or her own life, as well as for the life of the Church. Today many people who are not Catholics know that the Church could make a major contribution to our civilization, so they, too, ask that question.

This book tries to throw a little light on that question. It first recalls briefly how the Council understood the life of a Christian (Chapter 2), and then shows how this is deepening our understanding of Christian family life (Chapter 3). The next chapter gives a survey of new Catholic practices and thinking with regard to divorce as an example of how this new understanding is being (tentatively) applied in a difficult and important sphere (Chapter 4). We then look at how it is affecting the two primary sources of Catholic life: prayer and leadership (Chapters 5 and 6). After that, we try to get inside the attitude to morality of today's Catholic and ask to what extent we ought to be separate from other Christians (Chapter 7). Lastly some of the questions that we all need to explore are listed (Chapter 8).

It would be impossible for me to thank by name all the people who have contributed to this book, by their lives, their conversations or their writings. But I must thank John Coventry, S.J., John M. Todd, Benedict O'Donohoe, O.S.B., Gerard J. Hughes S.J., and Noel Landers who very kindly read through all or some of the typescript and gave me their criticisms. Any errors that remain are mine.

E.F.

1

THE END OF A LONG WINTER?

Someone who wakes up after a long winter to a sunlit day takes time to adjust to this new experience. The overwhelming response is likely to be one of joy and liberation. The world is beautiful and is there to be explored.

But part of him may be less sure. The long winter has made him less accustomed to a sense of freedom and exploration. He may even feel more at home with its restraints.

The Vatican Council announced to every Catholic that a long winter was over. No longer was the ordinary member to be a second-class citizen, or his liturgy to be in priests' language. No longer was the world to be distrusted or Catholic teaching to be the repetition of old formulae. The Spirit is alive in every Christian. This primary belief about the Church throughout the New Testament was restored. And the Spirit is the creative life of God.

So it invited us to recognize and respond to that life within us. But we had to work out how to do this in a world where we had had no experience of doing it.

How do I effectively help my neighbour to see the fuller possibilities of human love? How can the liturgy help me to be aware of God's presence in my life? Is it enough just to translate it into English and slightly modify the ceremonies? How can I share in the Church's developing understanding of God and his relevance to us, and how can I impart this to my children and perhaps to others?

Responsibility can be a means by which we grow as individuals, or we can regret it as a burden. Certainly the going became

1

increasingly hard. The Church had opened its windows onto the world and even declared that it had much to learn from it. But what should we learn? How should we discriminate between shallowness and truth? There were voices coming from every direction. At least in that long winter we were secure.

Some Catholics keep to the winter. Many have not been given a chance of appreciating what the Council was saying.[1] But there is a growing feeling that somehow or other the summer has begun, if only we could feel more at home in it. We feel that profound truths about Christianity and the world have inspired the Church to want for us a mature Christian life, but that somehow it hasn't quite found the way of providing it.

But, fourteen years after the Council, a way is beginning to take shape. The Church has had time to learn from experiment and reflection. This book is an attempt to describe what is beginning to emerge and to understand why it is doing so.

2

INVITATION TOWARDS SUMMER

The Vatican Council's understanding of Christianity starts with an event. God entered into a relationship with Hebrew people. Any description of something so extraordinary could only be an approximation; but the married relationship seemed to that people to come closest.

They called that relationship 'covenant'. At the most solemn moment of his life Jesus was later to use the same word about the relationship he was setting up by establishing the *new* people of God. He called it 'the new covenant'.

The interest of this covenant relationship for us doesn't lie chiefly in the fact that it was a beginning. Much more interesting is the fact that it showed *the way* in which God relates to his people. It is abundantly clear from the New Testament that he relates in the same way to us now. And since the whole point for us of our Christianity is to relate as richly as possible to him, it is important for us to listen to this first strong playing of God's 'signature tune'.

As in great music or literature or a profound relationship between human people, there are many facets to this experience, each interlocking with and enriching the others.

First it was an invitation to know and love. That statement can sound almost trite: until we realize how astoundingly it extends man's scope.

Of course we may know about or know superficially a large number of people. We say we *really know* a person when we feel we know the nature and the strength of a person's deepest motivations and attitudes. What human values does he stand for, and how strongly and how humanly does he stand for them? In other words how, at the centre of his being, does he seek to tackle life?

We *really love* a person (as opposed to just having romantic emotions about him or her) when we not only know that vibrant, questing reality that any human person is, but also see something marvellous in that person's way of tackling life, and want to enter into it so far as we can. My point here is that loving isn't just where I say, 'You are marvellous. I appreciate these lovable qualities that you have,' as I might to a beautiful picture on my wall. A picture is static, has no action. But a person is vibrant with doubts and desires, hopes and fears, loves and hates; some shallow, some deep; and underlying them and working in and through them all, and trying to grow and live as his or her true self is you or me.

Loving is sharing, so far as I can, with that complex action because the you that I have come to know there I see as marvellous. And therefore I feel, in so far as I can, for your hopes and hesitations and your deep desires. Through all of them you are trying to create your true self. Loving is sharing as intimately as possible, with mind, heart and action, in someone else's creation.

1 Sharing in God's *Creation*
Exactly the same is true of the relationship between man and God from that beginning to now. The only way to know God is the same as the only way to know anybody: through personal experience of what he does. And just as the deepest thing anyone can do is creation (in our case self-creation), so it also is with God.

This is what Jesus told us when he summed up his message, as Jewish religious teachers were expected to, in the form of a prayer. Our main wish of our loving Father is that his will be done. 'Plan' might be a better word, as we see in the letter to the Ephesians. God's 'will' or 'plan' began 'before the world was made'; its motive is 'his own kind purposes' through which

4

we can 'gain our freedom', our 'salvation', and 'live through love'. It is guided by his 'wisdom and insight'. It embraces 'everything in the heavens and everything on earth'. It seeks the harmony and fulfilment of the whole cosmos.

This is God's real work of creation. Not an initial shove in a remote past, but something happening now, at the very centre of everyone's being as we join in the common human task of helping to bring true fulfilment to people's lives. This is a partnership in which each of us is a senior, indispensable partner, and in which the joy comes not just in the work but in the partnership. We come to know and delight in the person at its centre, whom we experience as we share with him this work of love.

That, then, was the first aspect of this relationship with God, as it was at the covenant in the Sinai desert, and as the Council asks us to live it now. Later we shall look at the practical implications. But first we must look at the other aspects.

2 Sharing in the Actual World *(Incarnation)*

One is that in his partnership with man God has always taken not man in general but *these men and women*. He has taken us with our limitations: both those that come from our particular heredity, environment and upbringing, as well as those that affect all human beings. It is in *that* setting that man has found him and joined him: in the actual circumstances of our individual lives.

This became especially true when the Word was made flesh. 'Word' meant for the Hebrew the creative, effective and significant power of God, and 'flesh' meant the very opposite to that in our own lives: the fact that we move in our transiency to the total ineffectiveness of death. What John is saying is that in Jesus God took on all human limitations, even the ultimate one of death. This is what incarnation means: that God's fullest and richest creativeness operates in 'flesh' (*caro* means flesh), not in an idealized world but in the real one that we have to cope with every day.

5

This became clearest at the Incarnation, but it was God's way of acting with us from that first covenant. He chose a particular people and developed his relationship with them through the ways in which they felt and thought about things, and through the events that befell them. How else could even God communicate with us if we were to remain human? And yet we shall see that the Council's fuller recognition that God works with us *as we are* is of great potential importance for the more highly developed form of Christian life that it offers us.

3 Sharing as a *Community*

So far, then, the two aspects of loving partnership in creation, and incarnation. The other two aspects of God's way of acting with us arise from those. First, he acts with us as *social* beings. He didn't choose for his special purposes isolated individuals but *a people*. Today he acts through each one of us as members of his new people or community, the Church. Since God works with us as we are, and since we are by nature social beings who depend on others, this isn't really an additional aspect. But it has been so much undervalued, and this, as we shall see, has led to so much impoverishment, that we need to attend to it.

4 Sharing *with God*

The last aspect also arises from the others. The point of all of this is that we ourselves, ordinary and limited people, join with *God*. We remain Tom or Jane, Dick or Liz, but we touch and are transformed by God's way of living. St John makes clear, in his Gospel and his Letter, that when we love, we don't merely help with God's life in our world, God's creativeness among people, but we *live* that life. It is fairly well known biologically that a child leads the same kind of life as his father! Anyone who loves, John says, is a child of God.

We can say this to ourselves and believe it, but we shall remain to a large extent like the very young child who is told that his father has become king. We can get only glimpses of what it means, both for our futures and for now. But without those glimpses our Christianity dies.

In fact those glimpses are the adult's kind of happiness. We need the assurance that what we are trying to do with our lives has a deeper importance than we can grasp. This is true of all of us, whether we are Christian or not. But a Christian is someone who sees that this importance, this deeper dimension that we glimpse in our lives, is more than a general truth or a hunch or a law of the universe, but arises now and always from a being who can say 'I love you.' This is what we mean when we say that a Christian truly believes in God. It isn't a statement about an extra being. It is a declaration that the only way in which this Christian can make sense of what he experiences of life is by realizing that at the heart of it is God.

Hope for the Future
Let us take those four aspects of being a Christian and apply them to this question. Catholics who are aware of what the Vatican Council meant to offer us feel considerable disappointment at the long delay in implementing it. Yet our overriding feeling is one of hope. Why is this?

Because Christ promised to be with his Church always, and we believe that? Yes; but the hope is more specific than that. It is that *now* could be a special time in the Church's life.

I believe that the reason for this hope is that we have been enabled to know God better and work with him more consciously. A pious illusion? That can be tested only by examining some spheres of the Church's life today. We shall do this in the next chapters.

The test that we should apply to the areas we take must, it seems to me, be whether these four aspects of God's presence with us are coming to be appreciated in the Church's life and therefore applied to how it lives and acts.

Do we see Christianity as a challenge to come to know and love God by using our knowledge of this event-changing world, our talents, our enterprise, *in joining him in making it richer*? In other words, do we try to develop our loving relationship with God in the same way we do with others we love: by joining in his continuing act of CREATION: his constant striving to make the world become a better, more human place?

Next, do we do this in the way that he does: first by taking the trouble that he has always taken (particularly in the INCARNATION) of carrying out this plan of love in the context of *the real world of men and women* with their strengths and limitations; and, as an application of that, by remembering that *man is social* and that our Christianity is social: that we serve God as members of a community, a CHURCH?

And lastly do we remember that what we are involved in is an invitation to know *the depth and sublimity of God*? The main challenge of our lives is to grow in our knowledge of him, so that we may know him more fully hereafter.

Does the reader agree that if we neglect any of those aspects of God's presence, our Christianity is handicapped, while if we embrace them all vigorously it is robust and promising? If so, let us test them against what we see happening in the Church of today. This is the best way I know of charting the health and future progress of Today's Catholic.

3

FAMILY LIFE

It is certainly the case that in America, Australia and most of Europe, both in the Church and outside, the ideal of family life is much closer than it was to a personal sharing by the couple in each other's desire to be creative. This is because we have a fuller sense of the personal, and therefore, in many respects, of love. Gone are the days when it was taken for granted that the husband would be the Head of the Family and would cope with what were considered the more responsible and demanding tasks, while the wife limited herself to the household routine and showing affection to the children.

A husband and wife today are much more likely to see themselves as partners. Instead of occupying two different worlds, one inferior to the other, they are more likely to desire intimacy and a growing understanding of the aims and feelings of each other about the children, their way of life, their pleasures, the use of any special talents either of them may have, their relations with the neighbours and with each other's family, and the rest. Of course this desire can be weak or ineffective; but probably it is the ideal of most.

And this partnership aims more at a loving creativity than it did in the quite recent past. Couples with any knowledge of education or psychology know that a mother and father have individual and challenging roles to play if their children are going to have healthy personalities. A wife is much more likely today to be aware of her special talents and to have a chance at some stages at least, to develop and use them. Creativity, by whatever name, is a recognized expectation of life today, even though it may be spread more thickly in some spheres of a couple's life than in others.

This working together and caring about what matters most deeply to people is the best foundation for love. That we need to share this with others, particularly the family, is better perceived with the enhanced appreciation of the family and, in some localities, of the wider community. In the love, there will be some intimation of the sublime. What seems less certain is whether a sense of the sublime doesn't usually need the support and encouragement of others for strong growth: a need that, for Christians, worship is intended to fulfil.

Difficulties of the non-Christian

In the kind of married life, therefore, at which perhaps most people in our civilization *aim*, people's ways are very similar to God's ways. The non-Christian has little help in recognizing the similarity because he is the heir of a long tradition which *visualizes* God as living in a superior world. He will seldom have any encouragement through his imagination to discover that we are experiencing God in our deepest moments. To him the events in which God has so triumphantly manifested himself will have been presented, if at all, as 'just biblical history', rather than as a lighting up of our lives to such an extent that we want now to join together and celebrate them..

Married Catholics

To what extent is the married Christian in a better position to recognize that it is in his marriage that he can particularly find God? Obviously it will depend on what kind of God he is expecting to find. The fundamental question, I believe, is whether he expects to find a God within his experience or not. And what we must ask, as we consider today's Catholic, is the extent to which the Church is at present helping the married Catholic to recognize God in his experience of family life?

Let us first take a Catholic couple who are sensitive to a good deal of the developments in the world and in the Church but who so far have had little opportunity to work out their consequences or to see those consequences in action. Would the following be a roughly accurate portrait?

They respect the Church's official moral teaching, can get angry at criticisms of it, especially from fellow-Catholics, but feel it is unrealistic for them and people close to them to follow this teaching when to do so would harm people's lives. In such instances (e.g. in some cases of contraception, divorce and abortion) they feel they are on balance 'doing the right thing'. They may well feel uneasy at the same time for breaking the Church's laws but uncertain whether or not this is 'guilt'.

They are in favour, in principle at least, of a Catholic education for their children. The content and the methods of the teaching about religion may strike them as alien and even wrong. But they value the Christian atmosphere of these schools, and accept, with some suspicion perhaps, that 'these new theologians seem more acceptable to the young.'

They believe in going to Sunday Mass, though the fact that they don't actually 'make it' every Sunday doesn't seem particularly wrong to them, except possibly as a bad example to their children. How much they feel they get from the Mass depends on the occasion. Although they may admire the content of many of the sermons and respect the rites and the priest conducting them, they are usually not much moved by them. But they do feel that they get something valuable from attending. It reminds them of what gives meaning to their lives and of deep religious experiences they may have had. Especially if the service is conducted prayerfully, they feel the presence of God. Perhaps it is just for a few moments, at Communion, at the words of Consecration, in the silence between two prayers, or as a ray of sun lights up part of the church. But it is priceless to them that, however infrequently, they are reassured that human life, that can seem so cheap, has a dimension to it that Christians call God-like.

To What Extent is the Church Helping?

To what extent is the Church helping this couple to recognize God in his or her experience? God, we realize, is in everyone's experience. We know that the specific function of the Church is to enable its members to recognize this and so live more fully, for the enrichment of the world Jesus came to save.

It seems clear that the Church does help this couple to recognize God in their lives. Those moments, however infrequent, when they feel overawed and enthralled by the depth and tenderness of God, can colour the underlying aim of their lives. Their desire for their children to go to a school with a Christian atmosphere may get entangled with a wish for strict discipline ('thump him, Brother [or Father]') or overtaken by ambition for the child's academic success. But experience shows that a truly Christian motivation is influential in many and that it comes from an awareness that God is to be found in kindliness. In favourable circumstances, it results in a stronger appreciation of this in the family itself.

The centre of all this, the everyday life of the family, will, if all goes well, reflect the deeper moments and the couple's general aims for the children and each other. Anyone who has known a cross-section of Catholic families has often found himself humbled by the goodness of many of them.

Even with regard to the critical moral decisions that very many families have to take, the Church not infrequently enables the Catholic to find the presence of God in some degree. One example is contraception. Increasingly, the official Catholic position on contraception isn't the only factor involved in a couple's experience of this dilemma so far as the Church is concerned. Many (perhaps most) priests will tell couples who ask for advice to give serious attention to *all* the factors involved; and these clearly include not merely the official ban but also their own physical, psychological and economic situation with regard to their having more children. A priest's concern for the moral value of their lives (rather than for their merely observing laws) and his compassion for any difficulties they may have is for many couples a strong sign of the presence of God's love for them.

12

This picture, if it is roughly true of many Catholics today, seems to show that they do find God in the experience of their lives. The God they find is, moreover, recognizably the Christian God. They find him in their seeking for their family's good, in everyday family life and their general aims for their children. They may find him in the compassion of a priest as they struggle to make a humane decision in their moral dilemmas. In both of these they feel that they are involved in God's work in this world and that through this they know God, themselves and the world more deeply. In other words they experience God and his work as creative, incarnate and sublime. Here we are recording only the important fact that they are, however vaguely, aware of the real presence of God. In a moment we shall look back at the picture to see how much the present situation of most Catholics encourages them to use and develop this awareness.

What is certainly clear is that the community or Church dimension is indeed present, but tenuously. When in September 1979 Cardinal Hume appealed in person to as many schoolchildren as possible in his diocese for their views about the Church, he did this with conspicuous sincerity. Even so most of the young people found it difficult to accept the idea that they were members of the Church; and *they*, unlike their parents, have had the theology of the Council systematically presented to them. Both they and their parents will have heard in Church that they are the people of God. But few of them have seen this fleshed out in the reality of Catholic practice. In their experience, the Church is still 'them': pope, bishops and priests who make decisions, enact moral laws and direct the manner of worship from a standpoint that often seems remote from the lives of 'us'.

In what ways should the Church help more?
We can now look back at our picture. So far, except with regard to the community or Church aspect, we have focused only on the strengths. We have seen them to be of great value.

13

But the weaknesses in our picture are glaring. It is easy to see that they come largely from our failure to respond sufficiently to the aspect of God's presence among us that we have called community or Church.

This is clearest in two departments of family life: liturgy and difficult moral decisions. Perhaps the vast majority of Catholics simply take for granted that decisions on Catholic worship and on the Catholic standpoint on moral issues should be totally in the hands of pope and bishops. Their task, in theory at least, is simply to obey, yet it is *they* themselves (with the pope and bishops) who are the people of God. It is their discovery of which forms of worship help them best that should be the starting point for any decisions on liturgy that are really *Church* decisions. And they can discover this only if they are helped and encouraged to try out new forms; to use for themselves the knowledge we have today about how Christian liturgy can work.

Of course pope and bishops have an essential role to play in the decisions. Christ commissions them to be the leaders. But the purpose of the community of which they are the leaders is to assist the development of people. That kind of body requires a special kind of leadership, as any competent parent or teacher knows. It isn't possible to do it all yourself. The point is to help the body as a whole to do it. This means helping the growth of the members' initiative, confidence and responsibility, and judging the results discerningly when they have reached a point where they are ripe for that. Catholics have always rightly asserted that pope and bishops are the servants of God's people. But it is still often forgotten that this is the service they are called to give. They are called to give service to the life of God in the members of the Church.

It is the same with the difficult moral decisions. Here again the *chief* factor is not the decision of a Church leader but the growing moral responsibility of the members. I have to decide now whether to back an unpopular proposal at a factory or board meeting, to vote for a strike, to practise contraception, to divorce my wife or husband. To make a responsible decision I must get to know the probable consequences so far as I can.

14

In dealing with these problems for myself and in listening to what others have learnt, I can become a more responsible person.

Only *can* become, because how well we know and respond to the issues involved depends on whether our viewpoint is superficial and selfish (what suits my convenience at the moment, for example) or whether it really takes account of the full human consequences of our action. As we shall see when we look at the example of divorce in the next chapter, these consequences are profound and often complex.

The Church leaders have the same threefold function here as with the liturgy. First, they must try to help us look at the issues responsibly by encouraging us to overcome our tendency to stick to selfish horizons. Then they must remind us of the deeper human consequences that can lie in not being an active trade unionist, in practising or not practising contraception etc. From time to time a result of this process of shared experience and reflection will be that a kind of consensus will emerge. And the third function of the Church leader is to discern when this consensus has been reached and to declare this as a service to the Christian body and to the world.

Their declaration is unlikely to be definitive because morality is our response to human nature as we understand it, and we may come later to understand it differently. But it will be a most authoritative guide; for the Christian especially, because it will have arisen not from the deductions of moral philosophers but from the life of God in the community of the Church; and for others as well, because it will evidently have come from so much experience and honest and shared reflection, offered as a genuine service to all.

Everyday Life

We now come to the last of our three spheres of Christian family life: the everyday life itself. Here again we are asking one question: How could this be enriched by a fuller response

15

to the way in which God is with us, particularly his presence in us as members of his Church?

The answer can come only from the experience of those families who have tried to be more responsive. In a moment I shall offer examples from my own experience. It is clear, of course, that we're not looking for an ideal model. That would be absurd. We are looking for ways which families may, depending on their circumstances, try, directions of thought or action they may fruitfully consider.

We already know what directions these are. One is to share their search for a fuller kind of Christian life with others. The other is to help our fellow-men and women. Christ chose us as members of his Church because he wants us to share with one another and to serve the people around us.

Boston

My first example is a group I know near Boston in the United States. They started some years ago with the specific purpose of helping one another with the religious education of their children. There have certainly been problems. Sometimes there are strong differences of view, about religion or about the bringing up of children. But though sometimes painful at the time, even the differences have helped because they have brought home to the members the strength of what unites them and the variety of ways in which God manifests himself in people.

Obviously this experiment has encouraged them to explore the significance of their religion as well as ways in which their own and other children can grow in religious awareness. It has led them to try out different forms of prayer. Sometimes the families have a day in the country, together with prayer and, if possible, Mass in the evening. At the last meeting I attended one mother suggested that the adults should spend a day or two in retreat and consider whether the group should be undertaking other kinds of service. Perhaps they will decide that they can now use what they have learnt to help other families in the

16

parish. So far they have tried sharing, but the area of service has been limited to their own group.

The important thing is that they have acquired the basis for any developed Christian life: the ability to exchange ideas among themselves and with other people in deepening their Christian lives; the knowledge that service is joyful in spite of the difficulties, because there you meet God; the habit of reflecting together where the Spirit may be leading them.

London

My next example is from a parish near London. Three years ago two groups of about forty each were started, each with a priest leader. Once a week each group meets on a weekday evening to listen to the Word of God and reflect on it together, and on the Saturday evening to celebrate the Eucharist, when they also listen to the Word of God. This consists on both occasions of a member briefly introducing and then reading a passage from the Bible. After this any member who wants to makes his own comment.

For the first month most people didn't feel able to do that. The second month they tended to say something, mainly to fill in the embarrassing silences! Then they began to feel at home. By the end of the third month people really wanted to say things about the passage that meant a great deal to them. The shared reflection often goes on for two hours, not for discussion's sake, but because they care so much about God's presence among them, illuminated by that Word, and want to share this. Not yet with others. The avenue of service is still to be explored.

Newark

Back now to the U.S.A. this time in Newark. Just across the Hudson River from New York, Newark is the industrial sector of that city. It suffers from unemployment and ugliness.

In September 1978 the diocese started a programme whose aim was to help their people develop their Christian lives, mainly through forming small groups. The programme was to last for about three years. By the end of the first year 35,000 Catholics in the diocese were meeting at least once a week in small groups of ten or twelve people. The programme suggested once a week, but many groups decided to meet more frequently.

For a clear picture we need to appreciate the different roles of the organizers and the rest. The main difference was that the former naturally knew, before the programme started, what *kind* of contribution such a programme could make to people's Christian lives. They had learnt this by their own reflection (there was a year of preparation before the programme started). Its full significance became apparent only gradually; and they could foresee how this growing enlightenment could progress.

To do this the organizers partly used the means available: for example there was a full use of the parish liturgy. But everywhere where people are concerned to explore values deeply, whether in religion, higher education or in other spheres, the small group of not more than about twelve has normally been found the best means. There you get the stimulus of other people's viewpoint as well as the opportunity and challenge to give and develop your own.

So once a week these 35,000 people of the diocese meet in groups and listen to what God is saying to them in their experience, illuminated by the Scriptures. The organizers give guiding material that lead the groups through the levels of appreciation of the significance of God's call.

The first level is to know that *I* have been called. I am lovable. I am loved, valued, chosen by God himself for something that only I can do.

The other levels are where I gradually come to appreciate the significance of this. First, in a general way. Then as responding to God as Spirit—lovingly and powerfully creative in this world. And lastly appreciating how precisely *we*, as these particular people, can join in his work where we are.

No one forced those thousands of ordinary people to join these groups or to stay in them. That so many have voluntarily done both suggests that a Christian life based on a growing personal appreciation of the Word of God, on sharing, and on helping others is something that many find rewarding. To start it off we need help, as we normally do with any new and challenging kind of enterprise. But the purpose is not, and cannot be, to mould us into a particular kind of Christian, but to enable us to know the Spirit of God in ourselves and be led by him in the contexts of our actual lives: family, friends, neighbours, work and the community of the Church.

'A Hope for the Universal Church'

There is strong evidence that what we have just seen in Newark and those other groups is increasingly becoming a normal way of living as a Christian. In 1975 Pope Paul called these small groups 'a hope for the universal Church', and in 1977 the synod of Bishops called them 'a special opportunity' for the Church. Already in 1973 the bishops of East Africa had spelt out the reason why this is so.

> We have to insist [they declared to their people] on building Church life and work on basic Christian communities, in both rural and urban areas, because in them members can experience real inter-personal relationships and feel a sense of communal belonging, both in living and working.[1]

One of these bishops later explained the theology of those last five words. 'Religion', he said, 'must be relevant and effective in all the aspects of a man's life.'[2]

Most of this is recent. How soon other areas of the Church will follow is unsure. But one important thing is clear.

The Church is groping towards a time when families are encouraged and helped to enrich their experience of God with that of others; to nourish this on their own listening and response to the Word of God; and to realize that any adequate

19

response involves at least a desire to join in the Church's service to the world within an actual situation.

It is true that in England and Wales only one in nine 'practising' Catholics sees the importance of small groups increasing in the life of the Church (*Roman Catholic Opinion Survey*, 1980).[3] But we need to see this in the context of three other factors.

First, Catholics in English-speaking countries are seldom much in favour of what they haven't seen. When the liturgy was still in Latin, only a minute number of Catholics particularly wanted it in English. Soon after English was introduced, more than 80 per cent approved of the change. As the same *Survey* suggests, English Catholics normally judge changes by their experience of them.[4] Since very few have so far had an opportunity of experiencing small groups, it is remarkable that as many as one in nine sees their importance.

Secondly, the same *Survey* and other recent research seems to show that the Vatican Council's teaching about the Church has not been effectively conveyed to most English Catholics. There is little general awareness of what the Council was trying to say about the nature of the Church or the role of the laity in it.[5] As a result, there is little evidence of a yearning 'for a more prophetic, witnessing or challenging Church,'[6] and instead 'a fairly widespread and rather uncritical acceptance of present arrangements remains.'[7]

The third factor is that there are two kinds of small group. There is the kind involving ten or twelve, like those I described in Newark and Boston, and there is the kind involving a hundred or two. It is unlikely that more than a minority of Catholics will ever feel drawn to joining the smaller groups, with the high degree of commitment and sharing they require. But, as the East African bishops saw, the other kind of group (of a hundred or two) is indispensable in some form if Catholics are going to be able to 'experience real interpersonal relationships and feel a sense of communal belonging, both in living and working'—in other words, to *be* a Church. The very extensive failure in conveying the teaching of the Vatican Council to Catholics in England and Wales over the last fifteen years indicated by the recent *Survey*, will not be overcome until that happens.

It is in families and individuals who show this kind of response—and not just as an extra pious experience—that the vitality of the Church mainly lies. That the life of the Church does mainly lie in the Christian experience of lay people may be clearer if we turn to a consideration of divorce.

4

THE CHURCH AND DIVORCE

In the *New Yorker* there was a picture showing a man talking to a beautiful young woman. 'Alison', he said, 'will you be my *first* wife?' That satirized amusingly an approach to marriage. But since the majority even of divorced people take up once again the same commitments towards an exclusive, faithful and permanent relationship[1] it is clear that this isn't what people really want.

We know that as human beings we are capable of fidelity, of committing ourselves to another person totally. When a couple say at their wedding that they will 'have and hold' each other 'in riches or poverty, in sickness or in health, till death us do part', they are normally expressing their feelings not only about the person they have come to love but also about themselves: the grandeur of man is that kind of commitment; most people hope they are capable of making it and keeping it, especially now that they are marrying him or her.

Another generally understood reason why marriage should be permanent is the effect of separation on the children. There must be few adults who haven't had experience of or seen the short-term effects on children of the separation of the parents. The long-term effects on their own ability to form a satisfactory married relationship are more difficult to trace but are apt to be even more devastating.

The Christian has additional reasons for seeking permanency. Love, for the Christian, is sharing in the loving creativeness of God. It is joining him in his work of love in bringing our human world to flower, and in that sharing coming to know

22

his lovableness. The two characteristics of that lovableness that have been particularly experienced from the beginning of the Hebrew history are loving-kindness and fidelity.

What has been said so far is probably common ground for most Christians. A consideration of the general realities of human nature and of the life of the Christian as sharing in God's own life clearly indicates that marriage *should* be permanent and that this 'should' is of great importance.

But what should happen if the marriage as a loving relationship is dead?

Until recently that question—though poignantly asked by many couples—could not adequately be tackled by Catholics. Bishops and theologians taught us that marriage is a bond. It arose from the contract to marry, freely undertaken by the partners. Once that contract had been made and ratified by one act of sexual intercourse, this bond was something that existed independently of any loving relationship between the partners. The loving relationship might become irrevocably dead, but the bond remained.

It is easy enough to see why the bishops and theologians adopted this view. Guided by Christ's own statement on divorce and the Church's own tradition, they wanted to preserve intact the enormously important requirement that marriage should be permanent. In a society that automatically saw morals too much in terms of law, the Church inevitably expressed this within similar limitations. Now that we are much less bound by these limits we are able to tackle the question that couldn't even be asked when marriage was understood primarily as a bond: if a marriage is primarily a loving relationship, what should happen if that loving relationship becomes irretrievably dead?

It isn't just that we *can* tackle that question: couples are insisting that we *must*. In the past many couples found that a marriage where their love had died was painful or unsatisfactory, but it did not lack an *essential* element. Now that marriage is seen much more as essentially involving a loving relationship, they inevitably raise that question.

In a moment we shall see what is being said on that question of whether a completely broken married relationship must still be held to exist. But we shall understand the various points of view better if we first look at the developments in the last ten years in how the Church handles broken marriages.

How the Church now handles broken marriages
One way in which the Church acts is to **examine whether a marriage was a true contract when it was originally made**. It does this by methods based on the procedure of courts of law. The process is meticulous.[2] Since it has to be run by people trained in Church law, and there are few of these, there are long delays, which can obviously cause great hardship to a couple during what can already be a period of great stress. The system works at all only because a very small proportion of divorced Catholics make use of it: if they all did, it would be completely swamped.[3] The latest figures from England and Wales suggest that about 200 decisions are given each year.[4] In addition, many dioceses have insufficient priests available to staff these courts adequately. A survey of the United States in 1977 showed that 10 per cent of the dioceses were doing half the work and that most, if not all, the tribunals were hopelessly behind. The U.S.A. dioceses dealt that year with 18,603 cases. There are more than six million divorced Catholics in U.S.A.

Guided by the Vatican Council and Pope Paul VI, the approach of these courts to the cases they deal with is much more attuned to the fuller understanding of Christian marriage. Until 1965 marriage was defined by the law of the Church in terms of a consent to a contract by which the husband and wife gave each other the exclusive right to sexual intercourse. Unless it could be proved that one of them hadn't in fact agreed to that, the court was powerless to help. Obviously it is possible for people to consent to such an agreement while having a completely inadequate idea that married life is the mutual gift, not just of the rights to sexual intercourse, but of each other as a person. What the Church courts now ask, therefore, is whether, at the time of the marriage, a person had sufficient maturity to understand that he or she was committing himself

24

to sharing permanently and exclusively the life and love of the other.

The Church has clearly taken an enormous step forward in its approach to marriage. But two important questions remain.

First, *can* these courts adequately apply this new approach? On the figures given above, this hardly seems likely. Then, should the decision be made by a *court*? An increasing number of Catholics are coming to believe that it shouldn't. The Church is *Christ's* community, and in such a community members treat one another as trustworthy, responsible. It should therefore be the couple who *basically* decide whether there was a real marriage.

At the same time, they are members of this community. They should listen to the community and realize, also, that what they do has an effect on the community. In such an important matter as this, where the Church's witness to the permanency of marriage is involved and where advice from experienced people is needed, a couple who are seriously trying to live as members of the Church should listen to that community. The community, for its part, has a responsibility to its other members to tell them that the decision was a truly Christian one: that it was taken after consultation and reflection. But the community in a position to help the couple and the people they live among, is normally not the diocese or the region but one that is more local: the parish or deanery. In the locality there could be a team of people who would be available to help such couples in their problems by putting them in touch with other couples to learn of their experience of Christian marriage, of the thinking of the wider Church, of psychology and so on.

The second way in which the Church deals with broken marriages is in **allowing divorced Catholics to receive the sacraments**. The Church has a difficulty in allowing this because a Catholic who divorces seems to be publicly declaring that although his first marriage was a true marriage, it has now ceased to exist and therefore that marriage isn't permanent. But the Church considers it to be one of its greatest responsibilities to witness, as a community, to the fact that marriage *is* permanent. So how can it allow people who are undermining that witness to be publicly treated as full members, for example by sharing in the Eucharist?

The Church is increasingly coming to see, however, that the actual situation can be more complex than it had supposed, and that a simple exclusion from the sacraments needs further thought.

There is the situation where the Catholic is certain that his first marriage wasn't a true one but where this can't be *proved*. The Church's present practice of dealing with such cases only by means of a legal court means that present Church discipline holds such a Catholic to his present marriage and would be inclined to deprive him of the Eucharist if he departed from it.

There is also the situation of the divorced Catholic who has remarried and who is trying to live, with his wife and children, a Christian married life. He wants his children to value the Eucharist, but he himself is not admitted to it.

In that situation the Church is increasingly forming a policy of allowing divorced and remarried Catholics to share in the Eucharist when this can be done without giving public recognition to their divorce.

The third way in which the Church tackles the breakdown of marriages is clearly the most important one of **giving practical help to the couples involved**. Most Catholics have experienced a broken marriage of a relation or close friend and know the sadness and stress it brings. Often those concerned seem not to have deserved their fate but to be the victims of circumstances. Whether innocent or blameworthy, they need help, and Christians are increasingly realizing this. Often informal help is best, but organizations extend the scope. In America more than 24 dioceses established official ministries to the divorced between 1976 and 1978, and more than 500 support groups have been formed for them in the United States and in Canada. Compared with the numbers who are divorced, this is only a start.

When the Loving Relationship is Dead

We began this chapter by recalling why marriage should be permanent, especially Christian marriage. Then we went on to see that there have been considerable developments since the Vatican Council in the Church's understanding of marriage and the treatment of divorce. The fact that it now sees problems about marriage as bound up with a communion of life and love rather than with just a contract giving rights to sexual intercourse, enables it to recognize that some marriages formerly held by the Church to be valid were never really valid at all. Its greater appreciation of itself as a community of love and trust is raising questions as to whether the ultimate decision on an individual case of marriage validity should be in the hands of a legal court or whether it should be made by the couple in the context of a local community. There is also a growing appreciation of some second marriages of divorced Catholics who are trying to live according to Christian values.

It is in the context of these developments that we can best tackle the question we raised earlier: what should happen if the marriage as a loving relationship is dead?

Here we seem to be at an impasse. Now that the Church sees marriage as a communion of life and love, it would seem to follow that if that loving communion is irrevocably dead, so is the marriage. But the Church, and the New Testament, say that marriage is indissoluble. Are we contradicting ourselves?

One way of denying a self-contradiction is to say that a Christian marriage cannot die. Another is to say that the Church and the New Testament are not saying that a Christian marriage is in all circumstances permanent but that there is a very strong obligation on the partners to do their best to make it so. We shall look at how these alternatives are viewed today within the Catholic Church. This will provide one of the clearest examples of the approach to all aspects of Christian living that is emerging in the Church.

This approach is that of taking the teaching of the Church and applying it to our lives in a three-dimensional or incarnational way. First of all, how is the teaching of the Church ascertained? So far as the indissolubility of a Christian marriage is concerned, there would seem to be no problem. Christ says clearly in the Gospels about divorce; 'What God has united, man must not divide' (Mark 10:9).

But if we are going to be true to the facts, we have to take into account that this saying of Christ forms part of a wider picture. Two parts of it need our particular attention.

One is that it wasn't Christ's way to make specific laws. He was explicit on this point that he gave only one law: Love. This was certainly not permissiveness. Any responsible parent knows that true love for his children involves finding out what is *really* for their good and pursuing that unselfishly. But the command to love doesn't tell you how. It leaves that to you. It treats you as responsible and mature.

This was true of all Jesus' teaching. He chose the parable as his chief method, and the whole point of a parable is to help you revise your basic attitudes for yourself: to see God, yourself and the world more truly. Having tried to prepare you to assume responsibility, Jesus didn't take it away by giving you a list of do's and dont's.

From this it seems clear that when Jesus said about divorce, 'What God has united, man must not divide' he was pointing to a most important value, not issuing a command. He was asking us to consider most seriously how important it was that marriage should be permanent, but was not saying that all marriages, in our imperfect world, can be permanent. A Scripture scholar recently analysed the New Testament passages on divorce.[5] He points out that we have not only Jesus' absolute prohibition but also the exceptions reflected by Matthew's Gospel and those introduced by St Paul. He sums up the use of Scripture in this way: 'In reality the norm for Christian life and conduct cannot be other than the historical Jesus in tandem with the diverse pictures of him in the New Testament writings.' Jesus didn't operate like a computer where you feed your moral problem into the machine and out comes a text telling you what to do. He operated by living: relating to people and helping them in the situations they faced; and now he does this by living in his Church, as it, his embodiment, helps us in the different situations of our time. As a result, the Scripture scholar asks a question. Given that Matthew and Paul could, under inspiration, make exceptions to Jesus' absolute prohibition, 'why cannot the Spirit-guided institutional Church of a later generation make a similar exception in view of problems confronting Christian married life of its day or so-called broken marriages?'

We see from the foregoing that if we listen to how Jesus is really speaking to us, and if we attend to what has actually happened in the Church, we find that we *don't* have to say that a Christian marriage cannot die. All we do have to say is that we have a very serious obligation to prevent it from dying.

The Christian Moral Approach

The consequence of this is typical of the other moral problems. There aren't ready-made 'Christian' answers. Christians have to tackle their moral problems in the same way as everyone else: by a responsible look at all the relevant facts and by seeking the most humane solution. That in practice will mean being sensitive to the human facts and values involved and making a wise decision about priorities. What is specific about a *Christian* morality is that it has the highest possible appreciation of human values because through his response to them man can join in the life, the lovingly creative action, of *God*. Also specific to Christian morality is doing all this in the context of the Church as a community whose task is to promote that action.

So a Catholic couple is having serious difficulties with their marriage. What should they do, if this reasoning is accepted by the Church?

Both should try with all their powers to overcome those difficulties. Experts in relationships can often help a couple to see more clearly what is causing those difficulties and thus can help them to overcome them. Self-sacrifice is likely to be as important as knowledge. And the Christian has the strongest motive for that.

What if all their efforts fail, and it is clear to the couple that the relationship is dead? Only they can know those two facts. It is for them, not for a court, to make the ultimate declaration when they have made use of the means available of saving their relationship. Just as their marriage is of concern to the Christian community, so also is its breakdown. They should therefore inform the Church of what they have decided.

Are they then free to remarry?

Here they will have to consider all the values involved. A very important *dis*value of their marrying would be the example it would give to other couples. Many will be having serious difficulties with their marriages. Determination can often help them to overcome these. Such an attitude is apt to be weakened by seeing others give up the struggle. Something vital for the health of Christian and human society is diminished.

But there may be reasons *for* marrying that outweigh even as strong a disvalue as this one. One or both may, for a strong personal reason, feel unable to remain single. Again, only the individuals concerned can decide.

How Catholic Morality Can Develop

Divorce was taken as the subject of this chapter because it provides a good example of how today's Catholic is moving towards a more developed morality. If we look back at how the development in this area is taking place we shall better understand how it is likely to do so in other fields.

We saw that the first impetus towards this development was that the Church came to realize that questions about marriage cannot be solved by visualizing it as a legal bond. It is a loving relationship in which the couple and their children can know, love and serve God. The Church's stronger realization of this has come, as we have seen, from our contemporaries' better appreciation of the personal and from our better knowledge of the Bible.

This realization made it *logically* necessary for the Church to answer the question: What should happen if the loving relationship in a marriage is dead? What made it *practically* necessary was that the experience of married Catholics suggested to them that that relationship can be dead and that a subsequent marriage can be a valid way in which they live out the values of Christian marriage.

Catholics are also becoming increasingly aware that the Church's present way of dealing with particular cases of marital breakdown is inadequate. It is still based on law rather than on trust; it can cope with only a tiny percentage of the cases; and it is too remote.

What is in fact happening is that the vast majority of divorcing Catholics by-pass the Church's official structures. With them the official Church is attempting more and more to achieve a sensitive balance between two values. One is that it is the Church's duty to provide the extremely important service to the world of a witness to the fact that marriage should be permanent. The other is the fact that the second marriage of divorced Catholics often has most, if not all, of the characteristics of a Christian marriage, including a commitment to permanency—often much more than had the first marriage. It is obliged to balance these, *not* in order to make an official or explicit decision about the Christian validity of the second marriage, but in order to decide whether the remarried Catholic may receive the Eucharist.

Theologians are reflecting on the facts we have described. When the New Testament was interpreted just as a series of 'texts' rather than in its historical (incarnational) context, the Christian validity of a second marriage couldn't even be discussed. But now they are aware that the New Testament doesn't by itself solve the matter.

What is happening now is that theologians are drawing together these threads: the Church's understanding of marriage and its own function as called to serve the world; the experience of married Catholics and the findings of psychologists. In addition they are trying to help the Church as a whole to reflect on their implications.

What is *not* happening, however, is the contest so often described in the media. It isn't a question of a struggle between conservatives who are trying to preserve Christian values and liberals who would be content with their abandonment. The real debate is between those who wish to help the Church to apply the very demanding values of love, incarnation and the Church's service to the world, and those who see Christian morality as something different.

5

PRAYER

Many people today who adhere to no religion feel that if it has a purpose at all it would have something to do with prayer. This wonderful technological world of ours is much appreciated by most of its beneficiaries. But just at the time when we have rediscovered the mystery and depth in our personal relationships, the context in which we live seems to lack that dimension. So our little bit of the sublime, yours and mine, seems like a briefly burning particle, quickly to be extinguished in a mechanical, cold universe. Have we got it wrong? Is there in fact that dimension of depth to the universe that would give ultimate significance to our lives? Prayer seems to be the one hope.

In prayer, therefore, you could perhaps feel at home in the universe. The deeper your understanding the surer you are that our human nature is valid, has a glory to it.

Many young people searching for this reassurance from prayer turn to the Eastern religions. Often they come from Christian families. They haven't found in Christianity prayer of that kind.

Catholics and Prayer

It is by no means only young people who have difficulties with the contemporary forms of Christian prayer. It is well known that Catholics, for example, are largely dissatisfied with a great deal of their public worship. Much of it is saying or listening to words that mean very little to them, and the atmosphere often seems to them mechanical and half-hearted.

As was said earlier, religion does provide deep prayer for many, at least at certain moments. Simply by going to the liturgy one is putting oneself in a situation where many things can lead to prayer. Even the mechanical repetition of words can be a kind of 'mantra', releasing the mind from attending to the superficialities of life so as to pray.

There are no hard and fast generalizations to be made about people's prayer, any more than there are about their love. There are thousands of exceptions to every rule, themselves as varied as the kaleidoscope. One can only plot general tendencies.

But if the situation is roughly as described, a question arises. People today, of every kind of religious view, feel a need for prayer. Catholic public prayer doesn't adequately satisfy that need, even for the majority of Catholics. As the Catholic Church moves towards a fuller response to the Vatican Council, will it increasingly fill this gap?

I think the answer is Yes, for two reasons. First, the Church is now better able to understand what prayer is and, second, it is better able to understand how people can practise it. Since Christians have always held that prayer is at the centre of Christian life, and since the purpose of the Vatican Council was to make use of our deeper knowledge of the Bible and of human nature, it would be strange if that were not the case. But by looking at the evidence we shall, I think, see the most hopeful development of all in the Catholic Church of today.

First we must go back, with the Church, to the Bible. Its function, we know, is not to supply texts to support theories but to reflect in a special way people's experience of God. What does it show us about how we can experience God in prayer?

Prayer in the New Testament

Starting with the New Testament, it is clear that it was never intended to provide a collection of prayers. The Christian communities for whom these pieces were written already had prayers of their own. When prayers are quoted in the New Testament it is to help the writer make a point he finds interesting.

There are, therefore, not many prayers recorded there; but there are quite enough for us to see how prayer was envisaged, and they offer an extraordinarily consistent view of it. When we remember that these prayers came from a great variety of writers, addressing themselves in widely differentiated places and to a great variety of situations over more than half a century, this is especially remarkable.

Here is an example. Mary hears a prophecy from her cousin Elizabeth that the child in her own womb will be the Messiah. Mary's response is the prayer called the *Magnificat*:

My soul proclaims the greatness of the Lord
and my spirit exults in God my saviour;
because he has looked upon his lowly handmaid.
Yes, from this day forward all generations will call me blessed,
for the Almighty has done great things for me.
Holy is his name,
and his mercy reaches from age to age for those who fear him.
He has shown the power of his arm,
he has routed the proud of heart.
He has pulled down princes from their thrones and exalted the lowly.
The hungry he has filled with good things, the rich sent empty away.
He has come to the help of Israel his servant,
mindful of his mercy
—according to the promise he made to our ancestors—
of his mercy to Abraham and to his descendants for ever.
(Luke 1: 46–55)

What Mary is doing here is reacting with wonder, gratitude,

delight—reacting with all her being, to a realization of what has happened in her life.

If we look rather more closely at her prayer we shall see what she found so moving.

She sees this birth as typical of a person and his plan. Generation after generation he has used his power to do astonishing things for the people he loves. The basic movement of history was his loving-kindness and faithfulness, as it always will be. This birth would be wonderful because it would form part of that movement. It guaranteed that movement in an outstanding and tender way.

This prayer, in other words, expresses Mary's overwhelming realization of God's presence in that moment of her history. Not as a remote figure from a different world who occasionally communicates with this one; but as a person whose kindness and faithfulness permeate human history: of both the great avenues of political change and upheaval, and of a young girl in the Galilean uplands—as well as of yours and mine.

If we turn to the other two prayers in Luke's first chapters, we find the same thing. In each a person expresses wonder and delight at an overwhelming realization that in this moment God is with him and with the people he loves.

The same, too, of the 'Our Father'. In its original form especially, it starts with a cry of delight: '*Abba*: my dearest father,' or even 'dad'! This in fact 'says' the whole prayer. It expresses joy that at the heart of human life isn't emptiness or a vast interconnection of particles and forces, but a God who claims us as a father does his son.

It starts, then, and it also continues, like the other prayers. A mood of joy and triumph is less clear from its rhythms than in those of the others, but is surely no less demanded by what it says.

Next in the Our Father we pray that God's will be accomplished and his kingdom or rule come to effect. Fundamentally this isn't a statement we make with words but with our selves. It is what we say to anyone we love totally. I give my self to what in your deepest being you want to do, because in that I meet the self I love. This is the loving partnership in God's creativity, his loving action in everything.

This takes place in our actions in a human, imperfect world, by our reacting creatively and realistically to that world. This is impossible without an attitude of forgiveness.

We do this freely. The choice remains ours. We can let self-centredness (our only enemy now) make us incapable of this partnership. This, too, we face, in the context of our Father's love and power, at the end of the prayer.

Prayer, therefore, isn't our saying things to a remote person. It is our awareness of his presence in our lives and our reaction to that.

I am cleaning the house, going to work, getting through the day's tasks, or relaxing with the family or with friends. And I know that I am with a person who holds the whole world so as to bring it to the joy of light and of dancing. I know that in my chores, my travelling, my work, my love and friendship there is a dimension that I cannot at present fully understand but which at times I partly feel.

It is the presence of one who is loving-kindness and faithfulness and who delights in human joy. In prayer we feel not just the magnificence of the giver but the delight of our own acceptance. I am joining him in what he is doing. In the ways I greet the people I meet, in the way I treat what they feel and do and say, I am joining in that movement of giving which alone makes sense of life.

What will lead us to this awareness of God in our lives obviously depends on our character and circumstances. There are so many things that can open our eyes to glimpse the real depth and significance of life. It may be laughter and the love of friends, or the beauty in a face or in a landscape, or an act of heroism or generosity, or a simple, everyday thing like a ray of sunlight or a smile.

But what of suffering, evil and ugliness? Can we find God only in the good things of life?

No one has found a solution to the problems of evil and suffering, but a Christian can see something of the direction in which an explanation lies. The early Christians clearly had a very strong sense of Jesus' ability to share with us the life and creativity of God because he fully accepted human life as it was. This is what his incarnation meant. Not a gentle descent into a starlit stable but the taking up of life in the round, which went for him, as it goes for us, all the way from the love of friends to envy, misunderstanding, rejection, physical pain and death.

The human life that we know is a vocation to love, creativity and joy in *this* world where all of them are vulnerable. Christ and those who follow him know that in choosing to direct our lives by those positive forces we experience the fellowship of God. In our present situation, we have to choose them even with their vulnerability to the hatred, cruelty, greed and pain that can assail them. The greater our appreciation of the gift of life, the greater our suffering when those negative forces prevail over it. But for a Christian, they can never be more than the other—and at present necessary—side of what is supremely positive: the life in us of God. By accepting both sides—the whole human condition—I am looking for God in the only place where he is available to us: in human life as it really is.

In Jesus' reaction to tragedy, we see sorrow, fear, dread and repulsion. But we also see a refusal to be overcome by it. That refusal did not come from a cynical or even just a stoic acceptance of human reality but from an awareness of God and a trust in him. The characteristic of Jesus that stands out most from the Gospels is greatness of heart. Is that the real challenge of life as it is to the Christian?

But how can *we* achieve this awareness of God in our lives? In much the same way as we recognize the personal presence of anyone. To do that we have to give time to be attentive to them, and we have to become familiar with the way they act, their attitudes and desires with all that makes them the special kind of person they are.

That is why the Bible is so necessary for Christian prayer. It makes accessible to us the experience of men and women in which God has been met most profoundly and movingly. We find this as true of our everyday prayer as of our prayer with other people, whether in the Mass or on other occasions.

Praying with Others

Before considering the Mass, it might be better to start with a typical example of how people apply the principles we have mentioned to their prayer with other people. For this we can turn once again to the groups I described in London.

They meet twice a week to respond to the Word of God. Not to the *words* of God, but to the *Word* of God with them now, that those events of long ago can help them appreciate.

They are like Mary or Zechariah. In their situation now, with its responsibilities and opportunities, its loves and its fears, they see something of the grandeur and the intimacy of God's presence.

We have already seen most of how they do this. Some of them explore beforehand the biblical incident chosen. After a very short introduction (it mustn't limit people's responses to the passage), the incident is read.

What follows *is* a discussion but is so much more than that. To an ordinary discussion we bring our minds, and often our emotions, too. Our business there is to formulate statements.

To *this* discussion people bring their whole selves; the formulation of statements does help because they help us to understand things. But our deepest responses aren't necessarily in words. Here we try to bring the attention and commitment of our whole personalities, as well as our present situation with its problems and opportunities.

So there is discussion, silence, maybe music and movement. The atmosphere is one of shared celebration. 'We are involved in this together, and it is very good.'

Anyone who has had this experience understands why Catholics throughout the word are beginning to recommend small groups so strongly. In December 1978 in Notre Dame Cathedral in Paris a Declaration was read out from a meeting of the 15,000 young European Christians who had gathered in that city. It spoke of these small groups as being for many 'an opportunity to discover for the first time the freshness of the Gospel, and to overcome the gap between their faith and their lives.' In the same year the Bishops of Piedmont told their people that these groups are a special means of listening carefully to the Word of God and of applying this listening 'to the concrete problems of everyday life'.

The small group is the most obvious setting where this kind of prayer is being practised. But it is also being practised increasingly by individuals and by communities of religious, and above all it has always lain at the heart of how we pray the Mass.

The Eucharist

In the Mass, as we know, the main part is the Eucharist. To understand to what kind of prayer this invites us it is useful to start by looking at an incident related in the Old Testament.

Abraham was at this time very old. His son Isaac had no wife. Abraham sent his senior servant to find a wife for Isaac. The servant must find the woman God had chosen to ensure the fulfilment of his plan that Abraham's descendants should inherit the country God had given him.

God conveys, by a sign, his choice to the servant. That sign made the servant feel himself in the presence of the God of kindness who masters human history.

The man bowed down and worshipped God, saying:
'Blessed be God . . .
for he has not stopped showing kindness and goodness to my master.
He has guided my steps to the house of my master's brother.'
(Gen. 24: 26–27)

First we see a wordless reaction of his whole body as he bowed down and worshipped; then the cry of wonder and thanks; then—and only then—does he relate the fact that had

40

so greatly moved him: the perception of the kind and faithful God of history in that moment of his life.

This is in fact the earliest 'Eucharist' known to us. At the Jewish Passover meal, a Eucharist was said as the bread and later the third cup of wine were passed round. Like that servant's Eucharist—centuries before—they started with a realization of God's presence in that moment, then a cry of wonder and thanks, and then words that recounted what God had done, in order to reflect on who God is.

When in the largely Greek world a Greek word had to be found for this kind of prayer, the best they could find was 'Eucharist'—meaning thanks. But, as we have seen, it was so much more than that. Thanks is tribute for a gift; wonder is a reaction of the whole person, and here the reaction was to the total situation.

Jesus chose this kind of prayer as the centre for the covenant meal he asked his followers to re-enact. In the first centuries the president at the Mass would express quite freely the Eucharist reaction of himself and the people there to God's presence in *their* situation, which obviously included that of the Church as a whole. Now the Eucharist prayer has to be taken entirely from a book. As a result it is much more difficult to recognize that this prayer is *our* reaction to God's presence in *this* group of people. As the true nature of this prayer becomes more widely recognized, and as trust replaces fear in Church government, we shall be allowed to bring our own thoughts and situation to God, and this prayer will regain its intended function.

The Church faced the question very early on as to what would be the best kind of preparation for the Eucharist. The solution it adopted is still roughly reflected in the first half of our Mass today. It was based on Jewish worship in the synagogues such as Jesus attended in Luke's account of his visit to Nazareth. It went just like those prayer groups I described near London. Someone was asked (as Jesus was in Luke's account) to read a passage of Scripture that would illuminate the present moment of that group. When he had done so, the group

41

responded to what the passage showed them of God's presence among them.

Our Prayer

How can we make the best use of these readings from the Bible for our prayer? I suppose that most of us have some difficulties here. What solutions do people find?

Probably the chief difficulty comes from the fact that prayer, we realize, isn't communicating with a God who is remote from you. Nor is it talking with a God you feel near to you about a different world from this one—as though he were present only in the 'religious' part of your life! It's an awareness that God is present in this moment of my actual life.

But how can it be that for me? I may be deeply moved by those great experiences of God that I find in those biblical prayers. But how can *I* have that kind of awareness of God's presence in *my* life?

We know, of course, that a person's presence can be of two kinds: the merely physical, like the people who happen to be in the same train compartment; or the personal. We also know that we are liable to reduce the personal to the physical. We can forget the wishes, feelings and desires of a friend, so that he is no longer present to us as a person.

In our everyday relationships what greatly helps to save us from regarding a friend as little more than a physical presence are things like the smile in his eyes, his look of appreciation, delight or concern, or simply our awareness of how he or she conducts his life.

Of course as Christians we realize that God's presence with us in prayer is deeply personal. But realizing a thing isn't the same as appreciating it. A personal relationship is nothing if we do not appreciate it and feel it. If I love you, I will feel for you. In prayer we do not have the helps we have in our other personal relationships that enable us to *feel* that God's presence is personal.

So our prayer may be impersonal. Of course in our prayers

we will use expressions of feeling, like 'I love you.' We will say that we love God. But so does a child who hasn't learnt to know his parents but feels that it's what a child should say. We, too, will be sincerely convinced by what we know about God that we should feel like that. But the danger is that our actual experience of God in prayer is of a vaguely physical presence to which we merely attach those expressions of feeling.

What, then, are the helps, like the smile or the look of concern in our human relationships, that can enable us to experience God as *personally* present, so that our feeling for him *arises from* that experience?

It is here that the biblical view of God's presence in our lives is so important. In Chapter 2 we considered our experience of love. I suggested that we really love a person when we do not merely recognize a person's marvellous qualities but want to enter with mind, heart and action into what he is fundamentally trying to do. We delight in that continuing creation that is at the centre of every person's life, and we want to join in it joyfully and intimately.

Mary and the others whose prayers we find in the Bible had a feeling for God's continuing creation. It was deep in their nation's consciousness and came naturally to their touch. Take, for instance, their sense of his wisdom and splendour. In the events of their history, occasionally triumphant, often crushing and frustrating, they somehow heard the 'signature-tune' of their shepherd: the half-heard music of his wisdom and faithfulness.

But you could see those signs only if you looked for them where they could be found. As with love for any person, it was a question of joining in *that* person's creation. Real prayer can happen only when we are sensitive to God's creation: when we feel his presence in what he is doing.

That sounds like a limitation. Is it like forgetting your own interests and taking up someone else's for friendship's sake?

Instead, it is recognizing for the first time the significance and splendour of what we are doing.

43

How the Bible can Help us Pray

It is the Bible that offers us the most profound representation of what God does in the continuing work of his creation. In the experiences of him that it relates we can learn to 'hear' his faithfulness, his love, his gentleness and strength. But we will hear this only if we know the 'language' in which the Bible speaks.

I could, for instance, take the story of the Good Samaritan and read it as a moving and morally impressive story from long ago. It tells me that a man travelling on the Jericho road helped a stranger in need. It may prompt me to help others in similar kinds of situation.

But if I read it in the light of the Bible's understanding of how God acts, I find something of much greater significance.

1 First, it helps me to appreciate God's *kind of creativity*, which, if I am true to myself, will also be mine. The sweeping away of *all* barriers and categories (even the strongest and most long-standing that Jesus' audience could imagine) and reacting to a person in his need. That's life, true human life, then and now and at any time.

2 What I'm invited to join is also *incarnational*. The Samaritan reacts to the man as he really is.

3 The *community* aspect of the parable is less obvious, but strongly there. The parables were told in order to explain what Jesus was doing. He was forming a community of people who were open to his explanation of how God is present in the world. One day he would commission them, as a community, to embody that presence in the world.

4 We have appreciated what the story shows us only if it brings home to us, in the aspects just mentioned, the *splendour* of the God amongst us. Can't you see, Jesus was saying, in my eating with tax-collectors and prostitutes—in my sweeping away, like that Good Samaritan, all barriers and categories that prevent us from living as the brothers we are—can't you recognize in that the presence among you of *God*? Isn't that God's kind of

creativity? Isn't there something here that you can only worship?

This fourth dimension isn't something added to the others, but the effect of the others on us if we really see them. Since we have to choose words, I have chosen 'splendour'—but any word is a pale approximation. It is where, in a very concrete human event, we find our whole being addressed and challenged as well as met with a tenderness and support.

So prayer involves two things. First, we look at a human occurrence—because only in human history is God available to us. Then we try to recognize in it the essential features of God's way of being present. The chief feature (though it can be seen only in the other features) is that God-like fullness and appeal that Paul loves to call God's 'glory' or 'splendour'.

How We Could Make a Better Use of the Bible for Our Prayer
After we have considered what the Bible readings can offer us, we have to think about how we can enable them to do it. If they are regarded as 'improving texts' followed by some moral or theological deductions, we shall be ignoring their true nature and shall gain little from them. A Bible reading isn't just a handy quotation to illustrate a theme. It is the presentation of an event that can enable us to explore and celebrate the real depth in our lives. For it to do that we must respect the ways in which that can come home to us.

1 It must, for instance, *be* a celebration. We are embarking on something of exceptional joy and importance. That requires a certain mood or atmosphere as we begin.

2 Also it addresses all our powers, our whole person. It is to make us aware of the inexhaustible depth and love of our relationship with God and with all men and women. What chiefly conveys depth to us is symbol. It appeals not just to our mind but also to our feelings. Through these combined it offers us meaning, makes this radiant, and suggests further depth.

45

3 Lastly, the focus of all this is *our lives*. It isn't a bit of religious celebration or use of symbol for its own sake. It is where we come to know the significance of what we are doing and respond to that awareness.

What happens when we apply these three simple conclusions from our knowledge of the Bible to the weekly opportunity to respond to the Word of God in the first part of the Mass?

1 First, we are unlikely to have the Bible readings in the Mass as one item in a loosely connected chain of rites that precedes the Eucharist prayer itself. That part of the Mass doesn't just *include* the Bible readings, even as their climactic part. From the earliest times, it has existed *for* them. For our preparation for the Eucharist the Church didn't choose a series of loosely connected rites, but the fullest kind of Christian prayer: our response to the Word of God. We are much more likely to realize the opportunity the readings are offering us if we not only know this but also are helped to feel it in the way they are presented. Perhaps a silent prayer before a reading, or a brief introduction that doesn't treat the reading like a school-book, *telling* the people what to think, but helps us to be open to its meaning and majesty.

2 Equally obvious, but still more important, is the second aspect: *that in prayer we experience depth.* Prayer involves all our powers. Our whole person is in the presence of a depth and radiance of meaning.

Anyone who has taken part in prayer that meant something to them will probably agree that this is what we particularly remember about it. I remember the reflective playing of an oboe in a large parish church. A few slides, blended with music, in the candlelight of a common room. Most of us have our own memories, often as simple as that oboe. What is surprising is that they are still exceptional. Shouldn't one of the most obvious tasks in preparing a Mass or liturgy be to engage the *whole* person, mind and imagination? Instead, so often, it is either one or the other. We have a sermon, which by its nature has more to do with the mind. Or we have music, which may

46

not be all that relevant. As a result, even profoundly considered liturgies can have a disappointing flatness.

We need to rediscover the central importance of the imagination in prayer as an indispensable assistant to the mind. In a religion so essentially incarnational as Christianity, we cannot escape the responsibility of incarnating God's approach to us in the ways in which deeper meaning, in fact, comes home to us. We must, therefore, make a creative use of the varied and often simple ways in which this can happen—a candle in the darkness; a splash of pictures round the sanctuary, perhaps from the children; a slide or two, supported by music (necessarily in the Church?); a poster; a child or adult dancing; a mime; a poem; a silence; a short story, and so many other methods. Anything used for its own sake is a mere gimmick, and so a barrier to meaning. Instead these aids must be of a type that will help us reflect in the moments of silence (without which we find it difficult to enter into any liturgy), or to feel and understand what is being said or done, or to be aware of the presence of the people with us and how we are sharing with them in this experience.

3 Besides an atmosphere of celebration and the depth and appeal that come especially through symbol, the readings also need to be *focused on our lives*. That might seem too obvious to be worth stating, but historical circumstances have prevented our being adequately aware of this necessity and still more our applying it to how we live today. The removal of this obstacle by the Vatican Council is beginning to show us great possibilities for ordinary Christian life.

Above all it has shown us that the life of a Christian is fuller than we had realized. A Christian, we have often seen, is not just an individual person who obeys and worships God. He is essentially a member of a community, because the purpose of the Church is to show to the world the ultimate possiblities of human brotherhood.

The New Testament often speaks of Christians assembling together, and it gives a threefold purpose: the Word of God was heard, the people there developed their relationships with one another, and together they arranged how this community could offer loving service. They expressed their deepest response to the God whom they had experienced in listening to the Word and in their loving fellowship through celebrating the Eucharist.

Circumstances made it impossible for the Church to retain this threefold purpose. The consciousness of the people at Mass being a community called to loving service became obscured. So, too, did their taking an active part in coming to know and respond to the Word of God. In other words, the Word of God element was impoverished; the community part virtually disappeared; the Eucharist part remained, but was deprived of much of what had previously inspired this greatest of all human expressions.

The question today is how we can restore those three elements to their full interconnected vigour in contemporary circumstances. It is now becoming possible to see some of the steps that need to be considered.

What needs to be done
Perhaps the most obvious factor that we need to think about is size. How big should a congregation be if it is going to be a community? Of course that depends on the degree of sharing you want. Nevertheless it is an essential question because there is a number above which any real sense of sharing is normally impossible. There seems to be a general agreement on this among those who have experience of groups. Even with the most favourable kind of building and the most gifted leader, the number will seldom exceed two hundred.

From this rediscovery of the community element in the Christian assembly, and this simple but vital condition of size, several conclusions seem to follow.

First, the Church, in order to be true to its deepest nature, must restore the real possibility of community to all its members by having its weekly assemblies of generally less than two hundred. It seems true to say that the great majority of Catholics cannot benefit very much from the Vatican Council until this happens, because the biblical theology behind it presupposes community; and presupposing it and at the same time making it impossible is clearly the main cause of our present problems as a Church.

Community once being accepted as a decisive factor, what kind of Church would we be likely to have in a neighbourhood?

Since a neighbourhood usually consisted of some thousands of Catholics, each of them with different talents and temperaments, we might well expect that the most obvious feature of such a Church would be variety. There would be many ways in which people would want to form a Christian community. Some would prefer, at least for a time, a group of twelve or so. Here a fuller degree of sharing and mutual support becomes easier to achieve. The members can share their experience of loving service to those around them and make their prayer and meetings accessible to them.

Then there would be the basic groups of less than two hundred. In groups of this size the more regular members become aware of one another's talents and interests. Answerable to the individual members, and under the presidency of its ordained leader, the group as a whole would explore, in its shared listening to the Word of God, the kind of response it could make. Perhaps for a time it will decide to focus that listening on some social problem of the neighbourhood. The members might invite someone from the social services to take part in a discussion on the Sunday readings so as to help them to be more aware of the actual needs of people, as Jesus taught us to be. The recounting by members of their experience in serving the community around them will act as an inspiration to others to go and do the same.

Another assembly may specialize for a time in a more contemplative liturgy. Perhaps some of its members are musical, or skilful in visual aids, poetry or movement. If so their talents may be used to the general advantage of the group.

Another group may include a large proportion of young people who may find there a certain informality of style and an

49

ability to respond to their own kind of enthusiasm and problems.

Another may concentrate on helping people to understand and appreciate the beauty, depth and relevance of the way in which God has revealed himself in the Bible and does so still in the life of the Church.

The important thing will be that each parish, by its own structure, will be encouraged to experience, so far as it can, the rich possibilities offered by the Christian life, with everyone being able to contribute according to his talents and to benefit from the gifts and commitment of the others.

Of course it will be necessary to coordinate and control all this varied activity. The parish priest and his helpers will, like the presbyters in the early Church, be the conductors of this 'orchestra'. They will need to encourage, inform, teach, sometimes correct, and help both small groups and Sunday assemblies to remember that, however admirable their diversity, its value ultimately derives from their belonging to the one body. On special occasions they will give this unity public expression by having a common liturgy, perhaps with the bishop. And they will help the groups and assemblies to use the more specialized facilities that often only a diocese can provide, like specialist counsellors, educationists, theologians and others.

We must in all this always remember that the Word of God addresses us as the varied people we are in the gifts he has given us. Now that we are more aware that Christian life is joining in the creative power of God, in the varied circumstances and opportunities of contemporary life, a genuine response to the Word of God in our lives today must surely include those features.

6

CHRISTIAN LEADERSHIP

During the last fifteen years the Catholic Church has begun to ask some very profound questions about the purpose of its leadership. We know what is likely to happen when any body, large or small, asks really probing questions about itself. England, for example, started to do that in the last century about its educational policy. The result was that some major assumptions, on which much of that policy was based, were found to be false to the real principles underlying it. It had been taken for granted by most people that only the wealthier classes should have a developed academic education, that even among them the women would on the whole be excluded, and that such education should consist of a very narrow range of subjects. Once those assumptions had been dismissed, the way was open for an enormous enrichment.

Before the stage is reached when a body can declare that *these* assumptions are true and *those* are false, there is inevitably a rather messy period. Some condemn any questioning; some may see part of the way ahead; most have questions and suspect what the answers might be, but are unsure how these answers would fit in with their other beliefs. What we can do here is take some of these questions about leadership in the Church and see what light the Vatican Council and its theology can throw on them.

As a Christian looks at his own life, he knows that it should have something of the goodness of Christ's life. Most of us know non-Christian families who clearly have this goodness.

But we realize that our vocation as Christians is to follow Christ *consciously* and by doing that to help others.

Our Better Understanding of the Christian Task

There is no difficulty in seeing that that is our vocation as Christians. But what has started us asking questions is the realization that we have to do this *in this particular world*, with all the challenge of its actual needs and its considerable complexity. Through me as a Christian in *this* world people need to see that Christ offers the world what at its deepest and truest moments it wants to find; that at the heart of all life is a person who is lovingly creative in human life as it actually is and as it yearns to become. But is going to church and trying to be a good person in my family and my circle of friends adequate for that? If Christ cares today about the stresses on people's marriages, the unrest in industry, the drop-outs from society, the soulless neighbourhoods, would he want those who join him to tackle these things as the community that is his embodiment in the world?

We realize that he would. But we also realize that our present Catholic structures are very little geared to helping us do this. The position is changing. Great progress is being made in some spheres. But in general our structures turn our attention on our serving ourselves, not the world.

Simply from the point of view of manpower, this might well seem inevitable. The number of priests is small and is rapidly declining. In Ireland, for example, if present trends continue, in twenty-five years the number of priests and religious will have dwindled by a third, and most of these will be at retiring age.[1]

Visiting his parishioners' homes, preparing and leading worship, administering finances, raising money, serving on committees, visiting the local Catholic school and perhaps the hospital, is a full-time job that leaves the priest with scarcely any time for the training, stimulation and coordination of the Christians in his care to help them serve their neighbours. In fact we seem to be caught in a vicious circle. The more we come to see that living the Christian life involves serving the world, the less will dedicated Christians want to join a body which has to devote itself mainly to serving Christians. And as numbers consequently decline, it will become still more difficult for priests to lead us towards this new approach.

Impossible Requirements

Once we start to ask whether our leaders can cope with all the many tasks involved in Christian leadership, other questions arise. The most obvious is whether we're not demanding of our priests that they should be supermen when we expect them to be competent in so many fields. Some people *do* have a sufficient range of talents to be successful teachers of old and young, administrators, preachers, leaders of worship, counsellors and leaders of their communities in socially relevant action. But to expect that range of talents from most of us is obviously absurd.

We're not surprised to find that the priest in a given parish is a marvellous administrator, a kindly and perceptive counsellor, but casts an atmosphere of routine or even boredom over our parish worship. Or that, in another parish, the priest gives us a strong experience of Christ's presence through the way he celebrates Mass and involves others in the service, but is temperamentally unable to help us use this experience for the benefit of others.

All these facts force us to ask whether Christ wants all the main kinds of leadership in the Church to be vested in priests. In any other body of this size, we would expect the tasks to be shared out according to need and special competence. Did Christ want his Church to be an exception?

Rediscovering the Church as a Community

Before trying to answer this question, it is worth recording the fact that Catholics are beginning to ask another question that may lead us in a similar direction. Most of us realize our need for moral guidance. We know that human reality is complex and that our wrong actions can do great and lasting harm. Popes, bishops and priests offer us this guidance. We appreciate their reminding us of Christian values. We may not always agree with the specific actions they advocate. But we wonder whether the experience of the people who have actually to cope with the problems of family life, marriage, social justice and the rest should not play a greater part when the clergy speak in the name of the Church. Is it Christ's intention that truth should come from the 'higher ranks' to the 'lower'? Is the Church primarily a monarchy or a community?

These are obviously questions of great practical importance. They are also questions that the Church obliges us to ask. The bishops of the Vatican Council utterly rejected the view that Christ wanted his Church to be like feudal society with barons and ordinary people as merely subordinate. The Church's preoccupation since the Council has largely been to deepen our understanding of what Christ wants from his Church in this matter and increasingly to put this into practice.

The main evidence that will yield us this deeper understanding lies, of course, in what Christ and his immediate followers did. But also important, as we shall see, is how the Church of subsequent centuries understood and applied Christ's intention for his Church in the prevailing circumstances. That will help us to see what is fundamental in that intention and what is not.

Asking the Right Questions

As we start our inquiry we shall quickly see that it is a fruitful one because the Council and contemporary circumstances are leading us to ask the right questions. They oblige us to be concerned about the four aspects of Christian life. And we shall see once again that it is precisely those aspects that are central in this evidence. Here, then, are the questions.

If Christ came to be *lovingly and creatively present* in the talent, circumstances and dedication of ordinary Christians, is Church leadership sufficiently using those talents and that experience? Are the statements on moral questions made by Church leaders sufficiently sensitive to the complexity of the real world in which ordinary people's moral lives are *incarnated*? Should we, *as Christ's community or Church*, share out the responsibilities of leadership according to our talents, or should we rather expect the priest to fit into a normally impossible job-description? To sum up: is an inadequate response to those three dimensions of the Church robbing it of power and depth?

Christian Leadership in the New Testament

When we turn to the New Testament we may at first feel that we have wandered into a strange world where everything is upside-down. Our preoccupation was with very distinct forms of leadership (bishop, priest and so on); and we wondered whether more of the Christian community might come in. In the New Testament world there is a carelessness bordering on recklessness about distinct forms of leadership, and it is simply taken for granted that Christian community is primary.

Christianity *happened* when Christians came together to share their common insight into the meaning of life, deepen it through their common reflection on the Word of God and their celebration of it in the Eucharist, and used their Spirit-given talents in love and concern for others.

Leadership was obviously necessary. That was clearly Christ's intention when he founded his Church. But he laid down no set hierarchical forms. Instead, the forms they took were to arise from the needs of the local communities and the patterns of leadership they knew and felt appropriate.

It is of course quite true that this is not how we have been accustomed to think of the origins of Christian leadership. The commonly accepted view is that Christ instituted bishops, priests and deacons. In this view Christ laid down a hierarchy of offices as a structure of leadership, and Christian activity and life had then to fit into that. What today's fuller knowledge of the biblical evidence seems clearly to show is that in reality it was the other way round. The *primary* thing was the activity and life of Christians as members of Christ's community. The structures of leadership were to arise from that. Those requirements varied according to the circumstances of particular communities and the patterns of leadership they were familiar with. Hence the considerable differences we see in structures of leadership in the Christian communities in the first two centuries.

In fact, the New Testament writers give no particular attention to *structures* of leadership, since the right ones would be found by the communities themselves. What they *were* interested in very greatly was leadership itself. But this was something that everybody shared in.

To understand this we have only to remember how Christian activity was viewed. Its primary source was not from the implementation of laws or of commands from officials but from the Spirit, the creative presence of God, inspiring individual Christians and communities in their work of love. Each had his own gift from the Spirit. One might be gifted to teach, another to console, another to administer, another to govern. It was in this manifold, God-given vitality that the life of the Church resided. 'Since the Spirit is our life,' Paul reminded the Galatians, 'let us be directed by the Spirit.' It was from this, not from structures or officials, that one had to start.

Hence everyone performed an individual role of leadership. 'If your gift is prophecy, then use it as your faith suggests; if administration, then use it for administration; if teaching, then use it for teaching. Let the preachers deliver sermons, the almsgivers give freely, the officials be diligent, and those who do works of mercy do them cheerfully.' (Rom. 12:6–8) An inspiring picture of rich life with Christians as being called to act with responsibility and enterprise.

Of course you couldn't end there. For one thing, it was obviously necessary to coordinate this Spirit-led activity for the service of all. In addition, it was seen as essential from the beginning to ensure that Christian life would remain true to the experience of Jesus Christ from which everything had derived. Linked with that was the fact that very soon it became apparent that false claims were being made by people saying that they were led by the Spirit, to the grave danger of Christian communities. Discernment would be necessary.

But these tasks, too, were shared. First of all they belonged basically to the community. And in so far as the needs of the community required overseers (*episcopoi*, which we translate as 'bishops') or elders ('presbyters') these often operated as a body, sharing the responsibility. It was clear from the beginning that in spite of the evident necessity of people fulfilling this role, the danger would persist that they, rather than the life of the Spirit in the community, would become the animating force. God would thus be reduced to our own, less challenging, dimensions.

Narrower Perspectives

We see from this that what our experience of the present life of the Church prompted us to look for is in fact realized in the life of the early Church. God was found in loving creativity, shared among all, according to each community's circumstances and needs. This is of interest to us because we can recapture it. But we shall do this more easily if we recognize why the original vision became obscured. As Christ himself was, so is the Church incarnated in human culture. The cultures and circumstances through which it has passed have woven veils that hide that vision. Even today we are unaware of their presence unless we attend to them. The price of that is not just an inadequate understanding but an inadequate Christian life.

In times of war a government has to take powers, even over its citizens' liberties, that would not be tolerated in times of peace. The Church, as we have seen, was soon beset by heresy. Firm, authoritative definition had to be given to the essentials of Christian belief. Who was to do that?

In those perilous circumstances, the overseer (or bishop) seemed the obvious choice. By the second century, he was the closest thing the Christians had to a ruler, and if it were necessary to negotiate with the civil authorities he would undertake to do that. He would have been chosen as overseer as a prudent, experienced and probably educated Christian.

But it was like putting a businessman in exclusive charge of a theatre. In times of financial crisis, that might be a wise decision. But in ordinary times there are other skills that need to be given full scope. What was happening was that the overseer had now to combine three functions which had previously been distinct and which were seen as essential for any adequate community: overseer, prophet and teacher. This not only demanded of him a range of capabilities that few can attain to, but—more disastrously—it could also lead to the neglect of the gifts of prophecy or teacher, and hence to the loss of those essential dimensions of Christian life in that particular community.

Other influences were undermining the community aspect of Christian life, and therefore the encouragement of the Spirit's gifts to Christians. In a world of emperors and kings, the pull of monarchy was too strong. Even by the third century the bishop was closer to being a king than being a brother. At the same time, the Church was growing, and as a result the demands on organization. Bishops and presbyters were now becoming 'full-time' leaders. They were now the 'official' Christians. The rest of the community were the 'other ranks' who were expected to follow.

This impoverishment of the ordinary Christian's role was already finding expression in how Christians spoke about the Church. They spoke of 'the mothering Church'. This meant that the clergy cared lovingly for the rest. But it assumed that the clergy *were* the Church and betokened that the community aspect of the Church was receding.

An unobtrusive but very important change was taking place in the general attitude to the *qualifications* required for leadership. Earlier the only one considered necessary (apart from the apostle-witnesses to Christ) was a gift from the Spirit. Now the qualification could be considered to be the office one held. Just by being a bishop one was assumed to be able to exercise all the functions of leadership that the life of a Christian community required; and the likelihood was reduced of those gifts being sought where they might in fact be: in the community itself.

Today's Opportunity
What we are seeing here is that the richness of the original experience of Christ in the Church was too splendid to be retained fully within the framework in which people had to live and think at that time. Under persecution, many defended their faith heroically. They laboured under difficulties of communication far greater than ours. Very few Christians were educated—often only the bishop, so that the priest had to preach the bishop's sermon. What we have to consider is not whether they should have preserved more of their heritage but whether we, with many advantages they lacked, can and must restore it.

We, for instance, are now recovering at least an ideal of community in family, neighbourhood, industry, government and internationally. A barrier is being broken down that for centuries has prevented Christians from appreciating and being inspired by so much of what the New Testament offers us.

It seems necessary to insist at this point that our interest is in barriers not in blame, because over the centuries other barriers were erected. They, too, were probably inevitable, given the limitations of the times. And, as with the others, today there seems to be not only a possibility of their being removed, but a half-articulated wish and a practical necessity.

Priesthood in the New Testament
One barrier that we have not so far mentioned requires some explanation. So far we have described those who governed the

Christian communities by the titles of overseers or elders. These are the English equivalents of the titles used, at first in the Jewish-Christian communities and then universally. It may have seemed strange to the reader that we have not mentioned priests, even though the overseers and elders, and perhaps other leaders like prophets and teachers, presided over the Eucharists. Why have we not mentioned priests?

The reason is that in the first two centuries of Christianity leaders were not thought of in priestly terms. In fact this is far less surprising than it looks. In the view of the New Testament writers you needed a priest for your relationships with God only if God had to be approached through an intermediary. The priest's job was to be that intermediary: that is what 'priest' meant. But the whole point of Christ's coming was that intermediaries were no longer required. The creative power of God (the Word) and men and women with all their limitations (flesh) needed no bridge between them. The Word became flesh.

As a result, there are only two ways in which the New Testament applies the word 'priest' within the Church. First, *Christ* is a 'priest', now the only priest, because he is the bridge that makes any other unnecessary. Now that he has brought his people, the Church, so completely into God's own world, *the Church* is a priesthood, since its purpose is to show God to the world through our God-filled lives, to all who can see.

Later Developments in Understanding Priesthood
Eventually, because the Eucharist is a sacrifice, the bishops came to be called priests.

Priesthood, of course, meant not just being a mediator but also offering sacrifice. His profession was to concern himself with sacred things. In fact the Christian leaders were doing both. But the essential difference between Christianity and other religions was that for the Christian *this* world was sacred. Incarnation swept away the old understanding of the sacred belonging to another world which could be approached through arcane channels by specially appointed persons called priests. The sacred was here. So once the word 'priest' was used, there was a danger that the Church's awareness of God's creative presence should be chiefly focused on contact with a separate world. The leaders of a Church founded for the world might be seen as conducting their activities remote from the world. The incarnational aspect of the Church would become dim.

Unfortunately, this is just what happened. Not only was leadership already concentrated on the bishops and priests; but the power to consecrate the bread and wine was increasingly being seen as the *central* function of a priest. The way in which the Eucharist was eventually celebrated—in Latin by clergy only, and with the Eucharistic prayer inaudible to the people, further strengthened this impression that Christian leadership was primarily concerned with approaching *another* world through *special intermediaries*. Another strong influence was the tendency to neglect Christ's humanity, so that he could be seen as purely 'heavenly'.

The Price of One-Man Leadership

We have already seen the narrowing of leadership to the clergy. At first the damage was limited by a considerable degree of sharing. Until about the third century, the presbyters would in general be like the fellows of a university college. As a body, they would be the chief council for the Church and the bishop. In many cases, it seems, they would elect the bishop, usually from their number.

It was the same with the bishops. They governed the now greatly extended Church as a body, with the pope as chief among equals.

Again, the circumstances of the times eroded this community aspect of the Church. As priests had to move out from living with the bishop to remote villages, the remoteness and the primitiveness of village life helped to make the priests subordinate assistants. This took place from about the fourth century. The erosion of the community aspect of bishops-pope leadership was caused by later circumstances. The increasing turbulence of the times made reform in the Church essential. Strong direction was necessary. Communication was slow and difficult. One-man government seemed essential.

The price of this step, however necessary it may have been, was not only the community aspect of Church leadership and hence of much of its catholicity, but also the consequence we have seen before. The position of the pope, like that of bishop or priest, would sometimes be filled by uniquely gifted people who had most of the capabilities needed for their task. But apart from those rare periods you would inevitably have a leader who could not give what the Church wanted in some important areas of its life. He might have a keen sense of the Church's need for unity, but little appreciation of its being incarnated in so many different cultures, with the consequence that the missionary effort of the Church to a whole country or continent would be gravely undermined, or even destroyed altogether. He might be skilful at negotiating with governments, but not at helping the Church to apply its Christ-given insights to the world of his day. If he felt obliged to act as monarch, the fount from whom all government of the Church flowed, a considerable part of the Church's life could suffer from crippling paralysis.

This 'siege' situation, where strong defensive action seemed to compel one-man government, has been just as much the case from the Reformation virtually until today. The obvious 'enemy' was Protestantism, but the range was still wider. A negative attitude was adopted to new currents of thought and to many of those who were trying, within the Catholic Church, to exercise their Spirit-given gifts.

Stirrings of New Life before the Council
It was this situation that the Catholic Church started to change in the 1960s in the Vatican Council. The first signs of a recovery had in fact begun to emerge about the end of the last century. Many lay people felt that they had an essential part to play in

influencing the world by Christian attitudes and values. Popes Leo XIII and Pius X acknowledged the laity's right to help spread the Gospel and to take an active part in worship. But it was difficult for this to make any rapid impression on long-accepted beliefs.

But already two new factors had entered the situation which would make the Vatican Council's decrees possible and which are still yielding further insights. First, theologians were beginning to recover a better sense of the realities of human life in their study of Christian belief. Instead of deducing it merely from texts and philosophical principles, should one not see it as essentially arising from people's experience of God's action in the lives of men and women?

This meant going behind the texts to the experience reflected in them. When, for example, the Council of Trent had denied the priesthood of all Christians, was its intention to reject the belief that it is the function of the whole Christian community to mediate Christ to the world or to reject what it considered to be a false interpretation of the statement by the Reformers?

The other factor was, of course, the recovery of the Bible, mainly through Protestant research, as the chief source for any profound understanding of Christianity. For some time Rome treated this new factor with extreme caution. But by the 1930s it was beginning to have an influence on European theology. The Bible saw the Church not as a monarchy but as a community of people. Instead of a well-structured organization with nicely graded rights, the primary reality was real people in a profound relationship with one another and with God.

At first this immensely moving new insight into what it is to be a Christian tended to slide back into the medieval framework that the Church had inherited. When the Bible called the Church the people ('*laos*') of God, it meant the whole community of the Church.[3] Yet many still misunderstood it as referring to those 'under' the clergy. St Paul called the Church Christ's body, implying that all of us are fellow-members. But many still thought of the laity as being the body and the clergy the head. Yet even in the nineteenth century a theologian[4] had realized the importance of the biblical view of the Church as a community where *all* had been given the Spirit. It was becoming increasingly difficult for anyone aware of these discoveries to see leadership in the Church as the exclusive preserve of the clergy.

In the 1950s the life of the churches cared for by St Paul was coming to clearer view. It became evident that the life of the Spirit in them was too full to be contained by any structures. The Spirit imparts his gifts where he wills. The Church must use its official leaders to try to discern the genuine gift from the spurious and to coordinate their use for the good of the community as a whole. But that God-given life must always be primary; the role of the leader was not to dominate it but to serve in its use; and always there would be a tension between a power that transcends human horizons and the human limitations of the leader who must help to channel it.

Not that these biblical discoveries had much effect on the life of most of the Church at the time, and they were hardly known in English-speaking countries. A good Catholic wasn't someone who sought to use his Spirit-given gifts for the Church and the world, but someone who conformed to the well-tried ways and did as he was told. And a good Catholic leader wasn't someone who tried to discern and encourage the Spirit-given gifts of those for whom he was responsible if they went beyond or seemed to question the established paths.

One biblical discovery that was going to help before long to overcome this rigidity was that of the importance of service. Christ had come, the Bible made clear, not to dominate but to serve. Although even in the 1950s and 1960s a princely style of life was adopted with a good conscience by some Church leaders, an awareness of this discovery was growing.

By 1960 a theologian could say that 'the layman in the Church isn't a layman at all but a Christian,' because 'he collaborates in the active life of the Church, both in its internal life and its work in the world.'[5] Much Catholic teaching and legislation continued to ascribe to the layman a mainly passive role. But there were many theologians by this time who saw the Church as primarily a community where all shared fully, according to their function, in the work of Christ in the world.

The Council's Growing Understanding of Christian Leadership
When the Council began in 1962, it obviously would not burst
on to the scene, wave its wand, and solve all problems.
Throughout its three years most people throughout the Church
felt the Spirit was especially among us. But the Spirit works,
incarnationally, through our human nature. Long-standing limitations of view do not normally vanish in a year or two.

It was hardly surprising, therefore, that the decrees bore
traces of more limited views. The first was on the liturgy. In
general, it was most enlightened. In England, only four years
earlier, an archbishop had been appalled to hear that a congregation were being allowed by the parish priest to join in the
responses at Mass, whereas the decree now stressed every
Christian's *right* to take an active part. But the decree undervalued the biblical view of the Church, so that instead of the
Bible's great conception of the Church as the people of God,
there tended to be a two-layer view in which the 'people of
God' were simply non-clergy, with bishops and priests above
them. The fact that four years later Cardinal Bea asserted that
the decree really understood this in the biblical sense was just
one indication of what was really happening in the Council. He
was himself an outstanding biblical scholar. The two years of
preparation before the Council, and especially the three years
of the Council itself, had seen the bishops and theologians of
the world communicate on a regular basis, as individuals, and
in an atmosphere of hope. The Church was learning to re-
integrate into its life an essential kind of Christian leadership:
the task of studying and reflecting on Christian truth and its
relevance to today's world. The decrees reflect the *beginnings*
of that re-integration. They are doors through which the
Church can be led to a yet fuller understanding if that partnership is to be vigorously maintained.

The next decree showed a distinct advance. The Church is
'the new people of God . . . a royal priesthood. . . . All the
disciples of Christ . . . must bear witness to Christ.'[6] The word
'clergy' is avoided altogether by the decree. The Church is
basically a community. The different functions are to serve that
community. Special gifts are given by the Spirit to all. 'They

65

are to be received with thanksgiving and consolation, for they are exceedingly suitable and useful for the needs of the Church.'[7]

In other respects, too, the Council was achieving a more authentic view of Christian leadership. The community dimension was shown in its practical recommendations. Councils, involving priests, religious and lay people, should be established as far as possible in parishes, dioceses and in Rome to 'assist in the apostolic work of the Church'.[8] A bishop should regard his priests 'as necessary helpers and counsellors' and as 'his brothers and friends'. And 'in order to put these ideals into effect, a group or senate of priests representing the "presbyterate" should be established . . . to give effective assistance to the bishop in his government of the diocese.'[9] The full integration of the laity into the work of the Church was indispensable.

> The Church has not been truly established, and is not yet fully alive, nor is it a perfect sign of Christ among men, unless there exists a laity worthy of the name working along with the hierarchy. . . . Therefore, even in the very founding of a Church, the greatest attention is to be paid to raising up a mature Christian laity.[10]

A further advance was underlined after the Council by the bishops of Germany, Austria and Switzerland. The Council represented, they said,

> 'a significant change of perspective and a profounder understanding. The priest is primarily the messenger of God sent by Christ. . . . With this understanding the Council made a decisive step forward. No longer was he presented principally as "the man of the Sacrament" . . . His primary task is announcing the Gospel, provided this is understood in its fullest sense. It means not just preaching, but the whole work of bringing salvation to men into the material and social dimension in which men actually live.'[11]

The Council and the World

Another dimension of Christianity restored by the Council was an appreciation of the world. A misunderstanding of the Bible's apparent condemnation of the world had helped to lead the Church to hold aloof from it. Since the Church is a 'projection' of the incarnation, and since it was founded for the world, this was a tragic impoverishment. But the Council declared 'its solidity with the entire human family with which it is bound up, as well as its respect and love for that family'. It wanted to show this 'by engaging with it in conversation'[12] about its contemporary problems. Its approach wasn't that of a teacher who knows all the answers to an ignorant pupil. The Council acknowledged that, 'modern man is on the road to a more thorough development of his own personality and to a growing discovery of his own rights.'[13] 'It offers to mankind the honest assistance of the Church in fostering that brotherhood of all men which corresponds to this destiny of theirs.'[14]

It can do this because it has been given the task of revealing the mystery of God and therefore it 'opens up to man at the same time the meaning of his own existence, that is, the innermost truth about himself.'[15]

What the Council had done, with regard to Christian leadership, was to promulgate a theology derived from a careful study of the Bible. Above all it showed that any true consideration of Christian leadership must start not from clergy but from people. The only source of Christian life is the Spirit active in Christian men and women. The function of the Church is to be the community where this life is profoundly and effectively lived for the service of the world.

The problem was whether a Church that found itself with structures and policies designed for a different type of leadership could provide the community setting, the encouragement and guidance, that were now essential.

Difficulties in Implementing the Council

To what extent has this problem been solved? Certainly the general atmosphere in the Church has changed to one where many leaders try to share at least some of their responsibilities and where there is normally a toleration, if not a use and encouragement, of different talents. But statistics show that the problem has not adequately been solved in many places.[16] And fourteen years after the Council, it is possible to spot some of the obstacles that still impede progress in the English-speaking countries.

The chief one is that the Church in these countries has seldom tackled the central problem of community. In other words it hasn't evolved the situation where the ordinary Christian can develop his or her Christianity in the circumstances that encourage him to do so. We see this clearly if we consider the normal town parish.

The difficulties faced by a town parish in forming community are so well known that we need do no more than mention them. Because of its size there can normally be no question that the people feel that they are a community. As a result, however much they and the priest may regret it, only a few can feel themselves closely associated with *the specifically Christian life* of the parish. Of course they may, and often will, contribute money and effort to bazaars, raffles and clubs. But their number will make it impossible for many of them to feel that they can take an active part in forming parish prayer and worship or in showing the personal concern for others that could arise from them. That is for the priest and for 'them'. The present system almost forces most Catholics to feel that their part is to be passive recipients. And the fact that the form of the Sunday Mass is devised for them and imposed on them by some international body only reinforces that impression.

Yet the most elementary psychology shows that for a person to feel involved in a community it is necessary that he feel encouraged and able to use his talents in taking an active part. If the object of the community includes that of imparting teaching intended to illuminate his life, it will be of no use merely expounding doctrines from a pulpit. If they are really to affect his view of life, he must be personally helped to see how they throw light on the problems and values he has found in his own experience.[17]

When in 1977 Cardinal Hume and his area bishops invited all the Catholics in their diocese to reply to certain questions, their answers showed that very few were aware of the Council's most prominent teaching about the Church: that it exists for others, that it is intended to be 'a light to all people'. Most of them would have heard this teaching. But very few had had the opportunity of experiencing it in a Christian community where you could take an active and valued part in being available to the people around, listening to them, sharing your own inspiration and insights with them, and serving them.

Once again, then, the Council forces us to the conclusion that Christians are entitled to the *opportunity* to live **creatively** as fellow-workers of Christ in a **community** whose size and type effectively supports that. In such groups the life of Christ is effectively **incarnated** in the psychology of twentieth-century people who need to *feel* things that matter to them, not just know about them. It has also a much better chance of being **incarnated** in the neighbourhood, which may find it difficult to relate to a building designed for church services, but which is more likely to be interested by a creative, unselfish and open group of people.

Overcoming the Obstacles

It has long been obvious that the fruit of the Council will be much reduced for most Catholics until an *opportunity* to experience such groups as a normal kind of Christian life is given us. What has prevented it from being offered to us?

Some of the obstacles are inevitable. The churches and the bishops in the English-speaking countries had been very little influenced by the renewal of biblical theology before the Council. It was bound to take longer for us to allow it to enrich our vision of Christianity and to work out its implications. Nevertheless there is ample evidence that now there are few Catholic leaders who have not done so. Why do they not act?

The answer that would have been given in the past was that many Catholics had not had the chance to reflect on the Council and so were not yet ready for such a change. Such an answer is now less likely for two reasons. First it is generally realized that strong opposition to change comes from a tiny number of people who seem to prefer the romance of defending old fortresses to more contemporary occupations! It is also realized that the many Catholics who have had no real opportunity to consider the Council and its implications will be unlikely to have their misgivings allayed until they can see how they look in practice.

The real reason why the Council's teaching on leadership has been ineffectively implemented can be found in the Council's own stress on the importance of the local church. 'A diocese', it says, 'constitutes a particular church in which Christ's Church is truly present and operative.'[18] It will be truly present and operative to the extent that the community realizes that it, and not the Vatican, is the basic Church reality and so is encouraged to reflect on what it should be doing and give effect to its conclusions. But in such essential matters as ordaining the leaders required for establishing the communities it needs, it is not allowed to do so. It needs to ordain them to such an extent that it is being asked whether anyone has the *right* in principle to refuse them leave to do so.[19] The local church needs to know that its reflections on its experience as a community have a part to play in the development of the Church's life.

Over the last two decades the Church has been trying to awake from its monarchic slumbers in order to tackle this vital problem. There is a growing recognition that to do this successfully two things will be particularly needed.

A Shared and Open Kind of Leadership
The chief one is an atmosphere in the Church that we are a community of mature people sharing in an important task. It

must become evident to all that the fullest possible involvement is the right and responsibility of all. For this to become evident all levels of the Church will obviously need to act in this spirit. The popes since the Council have declared their wish to work in much closer partnership with the bishops. Whatever measure of success may have been achieved, this partnership will help create the atmosphere needed to the extent that there is a more open kind of government. The Council itself recognized the importance of the Church's becoming 'attentive to the developments in human relations which have brought about a new order of things in our time'.[20] It 'strongly desired' the department through which the pope must govern (the Curia) to 'be reorganized and better adapted to the needs of the times'.[21]

That the result of this would be far more important for the life of the Church than mere re-organization becomes clear if we consider its application to one department. As our example we can take the department concerned with preserving authentic Christian faith. Karl Rahner spelt out some of the implications with regard to it in 1969.

> We are deceiving ourselves [he wrote] if we suppose that the teaching office of the Church meets with more respect and trust on the part of modern man when it withdraws itself into a mysterious remoteness, when it conceals even the material questions with which it has to cope . . . when it prohibits a realistic and open discussion of the suitability of the theological advisers who are engaged, when it fails to make clear what objective and really relevant criteria have governed the choice of these, and when its decisions are not accompanied by any arguments, or at least any that do justice to the importance of the realities involved.[22]

We can see how that would work in practice. The importance of preserving authentic Christian teaching would be as great as ever. One of the Church's essential tasks is to give account as a body of what it holds about human life; and no body can do that if it cannot declare, '*This* we do not hold.'

What would happen would be that we should teach, so far as possible, as a body: a Church! This would mean that the

71

widest possible spectrum of Christian experience and wisdom would be represented, and the process of weighing these publicly shared. Since this process is concerned with a reality that eludes our full understanding or expression, the decisions reached in that process may often have to be provisional. Here we have to choose between the superficial comfort of 'knowing all the answers', which has no authority in today's world and no warrant in Christian tradition, and the creative community, incarnate in real men and women, where Christ is actually to be found.

The process would be guided, as such processes always have been in the Christian tradition, by the bishops (or their equivalents) and theologians. The spirit in which it would be conducted was expressed some years ago in a description of how a theologian, and any Catholic, would approach this task if guided by the Council.

> He has witnessed how Vatican II has gone beyond many doctrinal positions, some ancient, and some more recent, proposed by the ecclesiastical *magisterium*. (He) wants to remain in union with the Catholic Church. He wants to be faithful to the *magisterium*. He realizes that wisdom is given by God to the community. As we are dependent on others for love, so we are dependent on others for truth. For this reason, the Catholic theologian has learned to profess his positions in a tentative way, as questions, as contributions to dialogue, and he refuses to engage himself wholeheartedly in his own convictions unless he knows himself to be accompanied by the brethren, that is the Church.[23]

The manner of teaching described here was seen as necessary by the 1975 meeting of European bishops in Rome, at which the first main speaker was the present pope. It was generally acknowledged that the bishops need the theologians if we are to ensure 'that *in today's culture* the testimony given by the Church to Jesus Christ is the testimony of the Apostles'. And the theologians need the bishops if they are 'to avoid upsetting the faith of believers . . . and [avoid] running the risk of heresy'.

The two must work together in the service of the Word and of the people of God. This demands dialogue with the community as a whole. The *magisterium* has the 'last word', but this must be preceded by collaboration in the research in which the faithful are engaged.[24]

This kind of policy would have prevented much tragic impoverishment of Christian life. Even in the decades just before the Council many of the Church's most creative thinkers had been hounded and repressed. Teilhard de Chardin, for instance, had been forbidden to publish from 1925 to the time of his death in 1955.[25] These thinkers' work was eventually to provide the deeper understanding of Christian life promulgated by the Council. But while that policy prevailed, grave injustice had been done in the name of Christian truth; a whole generation had been deprived of much enlightenment about their Christian vocation; and, above all, repression and secrecy had greatly damaged the Church's witness to human brotherhood. The most certain outcome of the Vatican procedures against Hans Küng, Edward Schillebeeckx and other outstanding theologians has been to focus the attention of all who care about the Catholic church to see whether that dark night of the Church is over.

Obviously this shared and open kind of leadership is as much required in the development of the Church's action as of its teaching. And far more will be required than just the absence of unjust repression. The only purpose of the Church is to enter, at the deepest possible level, into God's creativity. The task of the pope and bishops is to help us engage in this tremendous task. The experience, thought and action throughout the Church can often die for want of means or encouragement or the inspiration that the attempts of other sections of the Church could provide.

Primacy fulfils its purpose by helping the churches to listen to one another, to grow in love and unity, and to strive towards the fullness of Christian life and witness; it respects and promotes Christian freedom and spontaneity; it does not seek uniformity where diver-

73

sity is legitimate, or centralize administration to the detriment of the local churches.[26]

Making Sharing Genuinely Possible

Our first requirement, therefore, is to develop an awareness in all of us that to be a Christian is to share, with all one's talents and responsibility, in a community's creative task. The second requirement is to make this sharing actually *possible* in the lives of all Christians. This cannot happen until the local church is able to be 'a particular church in which Christ's Church is truly present and operative.'

I remember some years ago a nun of mature years in a responsible position asking me what I thought about bishops' remaining in office for longer than ten years. I have to admit that I gave her an evasive answer. 'Role-play', she said, with utter and startling decisiveness, 'merely role-play.'

The assertion obviously came from her soul. I don't know what evidence she could have given for it. But that outburst did illustrate an *approach* that we shall need to recapture if we are ever going to have truly local churches.

She was tackling the question of what makes it realistically possible for a group of Christians to be and to remain a community involved in the creative work of Christ in the world. Whether her theory corresponds to the facts or merely arose from frustration with some long-serving bishop, is not the question. The point here is that her approach was to start not from the office or the institution but from what actually achieves the required objective.

All the bishops I know are immensely dedicated men who work longer hours, with shorter holidays, than most of us would consider possible. Yet I think they might well be the first to agree that they have an impossible job to perform. Not even the most dedicated genius can give tens of thousands of people a sense that they are in any cogent sense of the word a community. For a body of Christians to be a community we need at least to feel that we are working in the same field, which means a specific neighbourhood.

Until we tackle this problem, parishes will remain sub-departments of the diocese without the powers and feeling of responsibility necessary to be a local church. Hence we shall continue to have dioceses that are reputed to be the local church but can't be, and parishes that could be the local church but aren't allowed to be. In other words we shall be continuing to make it impossible for most Catholics to benefit from, or even appreciate, the community aspect of Christianity: to live, in any full way, as members of a *Church*.

The problem has been recognized for many years. Karl Rahner expressed it in a lecture in 1972.

> The focal point for the Church to discharge its function, to achieve credibility and to perform its task of preaching the gospel is now to be found in the local community at the roots of society, for it is here that its encounter with the special social situation must be achieved, here that faith must emerge ever afresh . . . in the old days the leader of such a community would be called a bishop.[27]

By our present use of the term 'bishop', he said, 'we have deprived the leader of the concrete community . . . of those tasks, powers and liberties which should really belong to him.'[28]

Obviously we would continue to need dioceses and bishops responsible for them. It would seem

> that the Church has been given the power to articulate the Church's own official ministry, which is ultimately *one*, and to break it down into specific offices of various kinds and degrees according to the demands of the time.[29]

This different kind or degree of bishop would be necessary for the work of the training of ministers, communication with national and international bodies, the organization of specialized forms of ministry, and general oversight. But he would no longer be committed to his present task of being a 'father' to impossible numbers of people, as well as administrator, public relations officer and committee man. The communities on the spot, the people in a position to do the sharing and serving, would have the main responsibility, so that Christian leadership can really exist and flourish where Christian life is chiefly required. So there would be different levels of responsibility and decision. But their true centre and focus would be restored.

Finding Leaders

But when we listen to the Council and seek to create these local churches, where do we find the leaders? The picture that has arisen from applying those four essential aspects of Christianity to our lives has been of a local church where the structures are devised, not by some inherited or uniform pattern, but to help all Christians exercise their creative vocation as members of the Christian community. For that it seemed necessary to have groups of varying sizes and aims, each with its own leader. Leading this 'orchestra' would be a bishop, who would no doubt share his task with others. In many parishes at present it is difficult enough to find laypeople willing to read at Mass or serve on the parish council. How could we find enough people to lead the variety of groups envisaged?

The Example of Newark

Perhaps we have enough experience of what can be done to begin to see an answer to that question. I have already mentioned the 35,000 Catholics who joined small groups in the diocese of Newark. This happened in an underprivileged suburb, by no means rife with 'natural leaders'. Each group consists of ten to twelve people, so that there are about three thousand leaders. This arose by the end of the first year of a diocesan plan for renewal. By then seven other American dioceses had sent representatives to find out how this could be done. Yet all Newark had in fact done was to make a full use of its by no means exceptional resources to provide something that anyone could feel encouraged to get involved in.

Their purpose was threefold: to know and respond to the Word of God; to develop 'vibrant faith communities'; and 'to reach out to bring the Good News to all'. To achieve this they used the kind of realism one would expect from an incarnational religion.

First, the planning was thorough and broad based. A year was spent on it, and active members of the diocese, lay, religious and clerical (the order in which they are listed by the diocese) were fully involved. Then skill and sensitivity were shown in recommending the scheme to the parishes. It wasn't just a matter of using the obvious techniques of securing its adoption by clergy and laity. In addition there was to be a strong and spiritual basis for implementing the programme. In each of the 200 (out of 252) parishes that adopted the scheme a 'Renew Core-Team' of twelve was formed. It consisted of at least one priest and of people both with and without a history of parish involvement. It met weekly for prayer and sharing scripture insights as the indispensable basis for what they were trying to do.

The scheme was gradual but sensibly persistent. Its main thrust came in five periods each of six weeks spread over two and a half years and moved from 'The Lord's Call' to a developing understanding of our response to it. The direction of the development can be seen from the titles of the last four periods: 'Our Response to the Lord's Call', 'Empowerment by the Spirit', 'Discipleship', and the ultimate aim (initially glimpsed, the organizers thought, by few) 'Evangelization'.

The next piece of realism was an intelligent (but open) use of the structures in which people can share their Christian lives. One of these is the parish. There was no attempt to canonize the parish in its present form. In fact the participants were asked to reflect on Andrew Greeley's view that 'local parishes as they now exist in the United States are much too big. Too big for effective worship, too big for effective social support of apostolic action.' But we must use what we've got. And for each of the Sundays devoted to the programme a liturgy was sketched out[30] that helped the parish appreciate the programme's developing teaching. Not just know about but appreciate.

Material is also provided for the other possible structures: home, the large group and the small group. Although all these are obviously important, these small groups of about twelve are at the heart of the plan because it is a matter of experience that that kind of size is most conducive to sharing. 'These small groups', the diocese said, 'provide a rare opportunity for us, the people of God, to share our faith; to listen more closely to the Spirit and to witness that God has called us.' There are something like ten to fifteen of these small groups in each parish, exploring what the Spirit is saying to them, gently being helped by the resources offered by the diocese to do this. An ecumenical dimension is at least beginning, since members of other churches may, and do, join these groups. Nor is their formation left to chance, since each parish priest is asked to commission people, including priests and religious, to find leaders. The sense of a lack of ideas so often experienced by small groups in their early stages is obviated by the fact that they feel part of a movement that embraces the whole area and have well-devised material provided.

In the context of that kind of movement, in which hundreds of ordinary people are involved, there is no great difficulty in finding leaders. It is certainly true that for the movement to continue and bear fruit, the continuing training of the leaders is essential. In Newark this is done between each of the six-week periods, when thousands of people participate in leadership training sessions arranged by the diocese. This means that all over the diocese, in the space of a year, there are lay people and religious acquiring the Christian commitment, knowledge of Scripture and leadership skills to help others to enrich their Christianity by prayer, sharing and action.

One of the things that particularly struck me when I went to inquire about the Newark programme was that it was a team effort, where everyone's skills were valued and used. A significant part of the team consisted of religious and of women.

78

The Role of Religious in the Churches

In any profound change, you need pioneers. Although all of us need to be that to some extent, the religious are the full-time specialists in that function (though by no means exclusively).

Religious houses used to have quite a lot in common with art galleries. People went there to live perfect Christian lives, and the rest could gain inspiration from visiting them from time to time and witnessing this 'ideal' life, separate from the world, and unattainable by ordinary mortals. You became a religious by vowing poverty, chastity and obedience. This made you quite different from anyone else. You were now in a world apart.

The other day an eighty-year-old nun told me that her order, which had until recently run only large institutions, now divided its members between that kind of work and communities of five or so around the country helping parish priests. I asked her which she would prefer to do. She said she'd rather join one of the small communities, if she could be of use to one; but she thought she probably ought to join one of the large communities 'to look after the old nuns'!

Religious have rapidly come to see that their vocation isn't just to *be* holy. Holiness isn't something static like a statue or a picture. Holiness is to share in the life of the Church, the community that particularly embodies the love and creativeness of God in the world. The vows, work and life-style of a religious aren't there to enshrine a private kind of holiness but to enable him or her to share in a specially full way in the ordinary life of that community.

The conversation I've just mentioned points to one example of that. Not long ago most religious orders would insist, as they always must, on the importance of community life. But their understanding of it was, quite naturally, that of the Church and much of society at the time. The stress tended to be on uniformity, following inherited patterns, and separateness from the world. Now what many religious are doing is *exploring* the creative and incarnational kind of community that is at the centre of the Church's renewal, in order to help it as a whole to see and to live it more richly. *They are community pioneers.*

79

Often they are also *prayer pioneers*. Their traditions, like those of the rest of the Church, can still lead them to confuse prayer with saying prayers. But many religious communities have escaped from that misunderstanding and are finding fresh ways to explore the depth and significance for us today of the Word of God. Their dedication to community life, to listening to what the Spirit is saying to the Church, and to Christ's love for people is an ideal basis for this.

It may seem odd to claim that religious are also *pioneers in obedience*! Obedience to religious superiors can conjure up a picture, even today, of the young canon who, in the 1920s, diffidently began a speech at a meeting presided over by his bishop with the words 'I think . . .' 'Think', broke in the bishop angrily, 'so you're thinking already, are you, canon!'

But religious obedience isn't directly about obeying orders, and it is completely inconsistent with giving up your own powers of judgement. It is to do with listening, as its derivation from the Latin for 'to listen' shows. Christian obedience means listening to God and responding to him in how we conduct our lives. The obedience of religious is sharing that listening and response in a community of people. Religious life can help the Church recapture the true nature and necessity of Christian obedience and its community dimension, both of which are indispensable in the local church, or in any form of Christian life.

Normally there will be a leader for this listening—though not necessarily—for some of the more mature kinds of religious communities find they do not need one. The role that a leader would play in such obedience or listening is described in a recent official study of Benedictine life:

> The abbot more than anyone else needs to listen to what the Spirit is saying to the churches: what he is saying to this little flock within the universal Church, and what he is saying *today*, not merely what he was saying yesterday or the day before . . . he must have time to pray, read and reflect . . . he must be sensitive enough to the Spirit to be able to receive effective inspiration from the present life of the Church and communicate this inspiration to his monks

. . . he should be prepared to recognize in members of his own community his equals or superiors in various fields, even in spiritual wisdom, and he should show respect for each member with his special gifts and talents.[31]

In bridging the difficult gap between past and future the religious orders can play an invaluable part. Many of them are doing so. Although they certainly have their own difficulties—like a high average age—the limitations in their involvement often comes from other Catholics who are unaccustomed to initiatives from non-clerics and particularly from women!

Women in the Church

The role of women in the Church is less a matter of the rights of women than of the rights of the Church. Christ works through communities. 'The church is church', as an African bishop wrote recently, 'only in so far as it exists and functions as a community.'[32] It exists to show the world the possibilities of human community. How can it do this adequately if it doesn't recognize in itself the complementary relation, as equals, between men and women? What can a community that fails to recognize that *say* about community to our contemporaries, unless it has for some plausible reason adopted celibacy?

At present there are still many departments of the Church's life which are like a family where there is no woman in the house. The house, and the family generally, lack those qualities that a woman can bring. Insights are not achieved, activities are not undertaken, the atmosphere is impoverished. Christian leadership is the Spirit in people, above all when they act as communities. To what extent are we entitled to limit the scope and human realism of that intention? May we diminish incarnation?

7

TODAY'S CATHOLIC

Successful parents know that they have to live *today*. It's no good treating your sixteen-year-old as if he were ten, or as if he were living in the world you knew at his age. The measure of your parenthood will be a love that urges you not to possess your child but to join him in his efforts to become more fully his true self.

A Christian's vocation is also to live *today*: to respond as fully as we can to the many-sided and demanding world we live in, and to do this in conscious partnership with the God who is love and faithfulness.

At this moment in its history the most remarkable thing about the Catholic church is the exceptional opportunity we have of fulfilling this vocation. Certainly, as we have seen, barriers remain. But we are increasingly recognizing that they *are* barriers and wanting to dismantle them.

What kind of person is emerging in the development we have been describing, and what kind of Church? If a Catholic takes this opportunity of letting himself be formed by the Word of God and living with the mind and Spirit of Christ, what will be his basic attitudes and what difference will they make?

All of us have to attempt an answer to this for our own lives if we are going to come to grips with this opportunity. Trends and theories are abstractions until we try to visualize their concrete effect. In the hope that it will stimulate better ones, here is an attempted answer.

Our Basic Attitudes to Life

We look at the world. We want to see it right. We realize that our first need is to relax. We have to let our defensive systems go. If we don't, we shall insist on crimping the world until it fits into our own categories and fears.

So we open ourselves to what it is. Many feelings come. There is the degradation and misery of so many. There is the craze for violence and the danger that our civilization may be destroyed by war. There are the selfishness, shortsightedness and superficiality of so much of modern life.

But there is also a growing respect for the dignity of the human person, and an awareness of the sheer wonder of love for another person. The media are helping us to break up the categories that divide us, as we are shown people who are different from us coping with life as we might. Our better knowledge of history and psychology makes us more sympathetic to people's weaknesses.

Perhaps above all we sense that we are at a turning point in our history. Let loose, so recently, into this industrialized world, we know that it could either make or break us. It's hardly surprising that over so short a time we have not recovered from the disruption of our community structures that industrialization brought and that we are still in the process of trying to forge new ones. But those new ones should have qualities that circumstances denied the older ones; they are clearly at the heart of modern life; they will be fashioned by you and me, or not at all; and many people have already given us an inspiring lead.

As he opens himself to this world and his place in it, a Christian has one overriding consciousness. Because this consciousness is a matter of feeling as well as of understanding, and because it has a richness we cannot fathom, it is best described by symbol. It is that 'God is light.'

At the centre of all that we know and can ever know is something that St John could best describe as the shining of light. It is dynamic, transmuting and invincible. It is the source of all the genuine 'enlightenment' we see. It shines in the darkness that we know so well, which cannot overpower it.

We are still looking at the world. To attend to God is not to turn away from it. We experience the artist in his work.

But in that work we also see ourselves. It isn't the kind of work that we can join as passive spectators. St John was quite explicit that anyone who loves takes his part in this basic action. A Christian is someone who *knowingly* 'walks in the light', so that others can more clearly see their way.

If I really know the loveliness of that shining, which I can see wherever human beings are trying to be themselves and especially in Christ, I will want to share in it from the depths of my being. All the time I am choosing the person I want to be. If I want to be fully my true self, I am trying to overcome what prevents me from freely making that choice.

If I am a husband, I will try to overcome what prevents me from being a good husband. There is the ignorance, allied with prejudice, that can deflect my love from my wife as she actually is, to a projection of my own imagination. If I do not know her inner feelings and fears, and her deepest wishes, then her life and mine do not mesh. Or perhaps I am too full of my own ambitions, desires or fears to listen to hers, or allow myself to be so set in my ways that her way of doing things seems unimportant.

To be fit requires effort; and so does it to be human. One of God's greatest gifts to a Christian is the conviction that that effort is worthwhile. Love as the supreme form of human expression requires the healthy action of all my powers, free from the blight of prejudice, distorted emotions, or imprisonment in habits blindly or selfishly adhered to. If I want really human relationships, I must attend to these. And I must take the trouble required really to know wife, friends or neighbour.

The Centre of Catholic Morality
But what is happening in me in and through all this is my adopting a fundamental choice about the kind of person I want to be. I want to fashion myself, with all my powers and feelings,

84

to live as part of God's enlightening—in my family, my neighbourhood and my work.

This is the continuing, never final choice that makes me the person I am and shall be. It is where, in freedom, I choose my course.

It is this choice of a fundamental stance that is at the heart of Catholic morality in so far as it is centred on the Bible. Sin is not primarily the performance of individual actions but a refusal to be responsive to human reality. And since for a Jew or a Christian the centre of that reality—its ultimate significance—is joining in the creative love of God, sin is a decision to reject that. It is accurately called idolatry because sin is where we make a fundamental choice in favour of something other than a life that is really God-like (say, just our own comfort, safety or ambition). By doing that we give ultimate significance to something that cannot have that. We are opting out of human life. 'If you refuse to love you must remain dead.' The Catholic teaching about Hell is couched in images that for many of us no longer 'work'. But all that it is saying is summed up in that final sentence of St John.

My chief duty as a Catholic, therefore, is to develop in myself a human responsiveness to my world. In the Bible's phrase, it is a question of my having a 'heart'.

We know that this is a difficult thing to do and that the cost of our failures—in terms of damage to people—is high. We are therefore in need of the help of other people's wisdom and experience. What have they discovered about our world and about how we can be more responsive to it? Whether Christians or not, they are our partners; though we have a special closeness and affinity with fellow-Christians.

The Role of the Church in Catholic Morality

It is in the helping me to have a 'heart' and so develop my fundamental stance to life that I need the Church. But here we must face the fact that the task of helping people be their true selves is a delicate one, as any parent or teacher knows. Instead of helping someone be more responsible, I am apt to try to relieve him of responsibility by drowning his self in mine. I might believe that it is wrong for parents to go on holiday without their children, to depend for peace on the nuclear deterrent, to support inflationary wage claims, to divorce husband or wife in any circumstances. If I make these beliefs into 'laws' and tell you that you will have a moral life only if you follow them, then I am not helping you to be responsive: I am telling you that I shall be responsive *for* you.

This is far from saying that my beliefs in these matters need be irrelevant to you. The alternative to making them 'laws' is to offer them as contributions to the common task of becoming responsive to the situations which have to be faced. Their value for you will depend on whether the situation you face is really akin to mine and on how well informed, enlightened and sensitive you think my response was. That will be its 'authority' for you: it will count with you to that extent.

Difficulties of the Church in Fulfilling its Role

The Church, as incarnated in human circumstances, has the same difficulties as any of us to achieve the right balance in its moral guidance. It has the advantages of its Christ-given insights and much experience of human holiness. But a long history brings the danger of encrustation; and leaders of large bodies are all the more likely to prefer directive to guidance.

As we look at the Church today, we see it struggling to surmount these limitations. To understand this struggle, we need to see what these limitations are. Basically there are two. One concerns the Church's understanding of what it is to be a good Christian. The other concerns its role in helping to form good Christians.

We have already seen that after a few centuries the ordinary Christian was seen as 'under' the clergy. As a result his vocation to Spirit-inspired leadership was forgotten. He was no longer the brother of all his fellow-Christian leaders, but the 'subject' of some of them: the clergy. In this hierarchical body, his duty was to obey their laws. Partly as a result, Christian morality tended to be seen as *not* breaking laws. The way in which the Sacrament of Penance was practised encouraged this impression. Morality, which is really concerned with our being most positively ourselves, could too easily be understood in a negative way.

Over the centuries, other influences increased this danger. Among them was an understanding of God more in terms of a person whose displeasure you must avoid, which easily led to the impression that morality consisted in not doing wrong rather than in trying to do right. This was very different from the predominately biblical understanding of God as one to whose loving-kindness and faithfulness you wanted to respond. Also there was a preoccupation more with what you did than with the kind of person you were trying to be, so that an 'examination of conscience' consisted more of concentrating on your individual actions than on how you were developing, through them, your responsiveness to God and man.

The Reformers' attempts to reform the weaknesses of the Church in the sixteenth century still further damaged the positiveness and responsiveness of its official moral teaching. The result was defensiveness and rigidity. Christian morality became a separate science that was expected to provide definite and generally uniform answers to all moral problems. It no longer arose from a reflection on our developing understanding of our world in the light of the Christian experience of God, but from a series of deductions conducted by clergy. In sexual matters their lack of direct experience was compounded by the distrust of sex that the Church had earlier 'caught', like a disease, from prevailing philosophies.

We have to remember that we are talking here about the Church's *official* moral guidance. Through the Sacrament of Penance and through the teaching of the clergy, it had great influence. But the chief moral teaching of the Church has always been through reflection on our experience in the light of our knowledge of Christ. Catholics were naturally much affected by the limitations of the official outlook. But they also met truth, holiness and sometimes heroism in one another as well as in the teaching and lives of many clergy, knew it to be inspired by Christ, and were led by this to love him and follow him.

The basic weakness in the official guidance was its lack of organic relationship with the reflection and experience of Christian people. If that relationship had been there, perhaps the Church could have listened to the valid criticisms of the Reformers rather than defensively rejecting them. What chiefly prevented this was the way in which the official Church conceived its role in helping to form good Christians. This was to tell Christians what they should do. A ruler instructed. Listening to his 'subordinates' was not his job.

Overcoming the Difficulties

As we look at the Church now we realize that it is struggling out of this mentality. Whatever else it may have done, Pope Paul VI's ban on artificial birth control made many Catholics conscious that *the Catholic community as a whole* has a vital contribution to make in resolving this problem. This has rapidly led to a sophisticated approach in the field of moral teaching among many Catholics. If it articulates the Christian community's mature experience of the Spirit in the lives of its members, then it has that authority. If it arises from a more restricted basis, that is taken into account. The mature reflection of any Christian deserves our respectful attention, because that is how God speaks to us. The reflection of a dedicated person with considerable responsibility particularly deserves that. But God speaks through us as we are. If by temperament I am blind to the evil of racial prejudice or the goodness of biblical research, then God cannot directly use my responses in those matters, whatever 'office' I may have in the Church, when I am expressing my own views.

The Church, in other words, is recovering its sense that it is a community of people rather than a hierarchy of rulers and subjects. But at present we are at a stage that is not unlike the private who discovered that the general was his brother. The problem is how to live the relationship in our actual lives. How can we share our experience of the Spirit without meeting to do that? This is normally impossible at the Sunday Mass in its present form. It would require reflection, sharing of insights and of interest in the practical results. Until we have structures that encourage all this as central to the life of the Christian community, the Church will be unable to offer us all the guidance it should.

Yet, as we saw in our chapter on divorce, a substantial start is being made. Surveys, ordinary communication and statistics can give some idea, however imperfect, of the consciousness of Christian people, though the lack of structures for shared reflection makes it more difficult to assess to what extent Christianity has formed that consciousness. Official leaders are finding more room for the moral experience of the Body of Christ in forming their directives, and many of them are deeply aware of its true importance. The international community of theologians are able to share the task of presenting the implications of these developments, in the light of the Church's Scripture and tradition, for our reflection.

The Old and the New Approaches Compared

As Catholics today, therefore, we recognize that the Church is moving towards an approach to morality that is more truly Christian. It follows so naturally from the biblical understanding of the Christian vocation that we can easily forget that this approach is profoundly different from one that all of us took for granted twenty or thirty years ago. Many Catholics have had no opportunity of seeing that the old approach is being transcended. If they reject the old approach as inadequate to their experience as Christians, they may believe that they are thereby cancelling their membership of the Church or are no longer entitled to full participation in the Eucharist. It is helpful to compare the old approach with the new, partly to remind ourselves where many Catholics still stand and partly to throw into clearer relief what has already been said. To do this we shall make four comparisons:

1 The older approach viewed morality as directives received from *outside* yourself, whether from God, the Church, the State, or elsewhere. Morality was, therefore, a question of obeying these directives.

The new approach sees *any* adequate morality as something arising from *within* each person. To become more moral means growing lovingly more responsive to the human reality that concerns me. *Christian* morality is the same as that, except that the Christian has far greater incentive and support in wanting to be lovingly responsive because he knows that by doing so he is coming to know and love God, joining him in his work of bringing light to the world.

In the older approach the responsibility for shaping my morality belonged to *others*. In the new approach, it belongs primarily to *myself*, because God wants me to become as fully human as I can, and therefore responsible, mature, loving.

Although the new approach doesn't see morality as chiefly consisting in obeying laws or specific teaching, it recognizes the value of these. So far as *laws* are concerned, any body needs to indicate the kind of conduct considered necessary for that body to achieve its aims by making disciplinary laws—as a football club must control the entry rules for its football ground. So far as *teaching* is concerned, the Church is commissioned by Christ to teach his truth. But here we have to remember that there are various kinds of moral teaching. There is the kind that relieves me of my responsibility and there is the kind whose chief aim is to foster it. Since the latter is Christ's paramount wish for me, it must also be the Church's. How, then, should I use the Church's moral teaching so that it helps me to be more responsive?

How the Church's Moral Teaching Should be Used
Once again the answer lies in our remembering the four ways in which Christ is present to us. So far as the *Church's teaching*

is concerned (coming later to how I receive it), the Spirit or *creative power* of God is acting through it, and therefore a Christian should deeply respect it. This respect would normally lead to the following of its guidance. The Spirit acts through people, *incarnated* in the strengths and limitations both of their times and of their individual personalities. Although the first Vatican Council (1870) seems to have taught that the Church can in principle transcend these limitations by teaching infallibly about morals, the Church has never claimed to have done so. A Christian should therefore realize that the Church's moral teaching is liable to error. The Spirit acts through the Church *as a community*; therefore the more the teaching arises from the reflection of the community, the greater its authority.

The Spirit is also present in the same four ways in the individual Christian *as he receives this teaching*, as he listens to it and has to make the actual moral decision. Each of the four ways is clearly important for him, but perhaps the incarnational way requires some comment.

The purpose of moral teaching is, of course, to enlighten moral action. But moral actions are undertaken by people; every person and his or her circumstances have their own distinctive features; and therefore these must be taken into full account before we can tell whether a particular action is right or wrong.

An Example

Suppose a couple are considering whether to put their severely handicapped child into a home. If this is to be a decision that is really responsive to that particular human situation (and so be a *moral* decision), it will have to take full account of all the human values involved. Obvious values will be the goodness of a happy family life for children; the special help a home can give the handicapped; the benefits a family derives from caring for a handicapped member; the mother's need not to be strained beyond her strength, both for her sake and that of the family's. No doubt there will be other important values too.

Each particular case will have a different set of values, and the balance between them will be different. The Church's moral teaching will normally throw much light on those values. But the Church does not, and cannot, attempt to assess where, in this particular case, the balance between them lies. That is the task of the couple. The moral life of the Church is ultimately incarnated in the responsible decisions of its members.

Aren't Some Actions Specifically Forbidden?

But aren't there *some* actions that are specifically forbidden or commanded by the Church, apart from its disciplinary laws? The Ten Commandments and other parts of the Old and New Testaments insist that some actions should be done or avoided. Surely actions like murder and lying are always wrong? And haven't abortion, pre-marital sex and artificial contraception been consistently condemned by the Church?

The objection with regard to the Bible has already been partly met. Jesus does seem to have absolutely proscribed divorce, and the New Testament itself shows us that the Church applied the light Jesus was shedding on this matter to the different situations of a later time and as a result made some exceptions. Once again, the Spirit has always worked through *people*, who are incarnated in a particular time and situation. Of course we can learn from them; but not by uncritically applying their words to what may be a different situation. St Paul's words that women should not teach in public or make any contributions of their own at Christian assemblies are enough to alert us to that fact.

But what of the Ten Commandments? Surely these apply to all situations? In fact, though, even a superficial glance at them shows us that virtually all Christians have always believed that one of them doesn't apply to all situations. The Commandment 'You shall not kill' is conscientiously broken in cases of self-defence, war and capital punishment.

Scholars have shown us the purpose of the Ten Commandments as we have them. They were the marriage vows of Israel with God, her husband. They were proclaimed as part of a liturgy that solemnly renewed those vows. They were a commitment of obedience, not to a static list of rules, but to a God of power and mystery whom they had found to transcend all such human categories. So the central part of the proclamation was the community's commitment to God. The other Commandments indicated their desire to live good lives in loving obedience to their God. This was indicated by a selection of concrete moral requirements from other Middle East cultures. The selection wasn't a particularly enlightened one (for example the Fifth Commandment prohibited killing only within the community). But then it wasn't intended to be. They weren't meant to be a full description of a moral life, but a symbol of loving commitment in which the whole people could share. The full practical consequences of that commitment would always have to be worked out by this people and individuals in their changing histories.

The objection that actions like murder and lying are always forbidden by the Church is quickly answered. When I tell you that murder is wrong I am not telling you how you should act in a particular situation. You may be grateful to me for reminding you that murder is evil; but you still have the problem of deciding whether this particular killing would be wrong. If you decide it would be, only *then* is it for you an act of murder. Murder means wrongful killing, just as lying means wrongfully deceiving someone. They are labels that we can apply only *after* we have assessed a particular action. The Church does us an important service by reminding us of the great evil that label points to. But once again it is enlightening us about values, not taking our actual decision.

What, then, of actions like abortion, contraception, pre-marital sex and divorce? It is certainly true that the older approach to Catholic morality held that these specific actions were of their very nature forbidden. Is this different in the new approach? If so, does this conflict with the official teaching of the Church?

We have already seen in the case of divorce that the new approach would not tell a married person that he or she should not divorce on the grounds that divorce is *necessarily always* wrong. It would say that divorce brings great harm: a fact that any thinking adult is aware of. Divorce is likely to damage one of the most important values of human society—one on which the very fabric of human society depends. It will also be likely to undermine the Church's witness to that value. But if now there is really no reasonable possibility of a loving relationship between the couple, those other values must be balanced against this disvalue, in the context of the loving support and witness of the Church. Once again, then, the Church is trying to help us appreciate moral values, not to make the decisions for us.

The official teaching of the Church seems to take a different view. Pope John Paul II recently endorsed the view that 'Christian marriage is as indissoluble and irrevocable as God's love for his people' and ratified Pope Paul VI's condemnation of artificial contraception.[2] In such statements the official teaching *may* be saying that if one does balance the human values concerned in any actual decision on such matters, it could in no conceivable case be right to have an abortion, practise artificial contraception, have pre-marital sex or institute divorce; or it may be saying that even if performing one of those actions in a given case would do less harm than not doing it, it would be evil of its very nature irrespective of the harm it would do, and therefore should never be performed.

If it is saying the latter, then we have a conflict of view between the official teaching on the one hand and a growing number of the best Catholic moral theologians on the other, as well as the other Christian churches and the moral approach of many non-Christians. This evidently calls for an exchange of views. What would have to be asked then would be why actions like divorce should demand this different approach.

What is clear about the official teaching is that it is stressing some values that are fundamental to human life. Here it is offering an essential service to our age. What is not at present clear is whether it is offering it in such a way that our age can benefit from it. If it were to stress that taking innocent life, practising artificial contraception irresponsibly, or undermining

94

the permanence of marriage does grave harm, it would be saying things that our age can appreciate and greatly needs to hear. But when it says that abortion, artificial contraception and divorce are wrong, this tends to convey to people that there is a special set of moral laws for Catholics whose basis and approach are unclear.

2 The second way in which the new approach is different from the old is akin to the first. In the old approach morality tended to be seen primarily as performing or avoiding certain actions. In the new it is seen primarily as enabling a person to become as responsive as possible to human values. Obviously our actions are the means and the expression of our development as individuals. Only by actually joining in God's work of love (and avoiding what undermines that) can I come to know what love is, what God is, what human beings—including myself— should be. I can become responsive only by living responsibly. It is with that growing commitment to being responsive that morality is primarily concerned.

3 The new approach not only stresses the fact that morality consists of our joining in God's work in the actual circumstances of our lives (the *creative* and *incarnational* dimensions), but also that a Christian morality should find much of its nourishment and inspiration in our life within the Christian *community*. The older approach was equally insistent on our deriving inspiration and support from the example of other Christians. But to this the new approach would add two elements. One is the importance of acting so far as possible with people who really share with one another, and with others, in our service to the world. Hence the growing importance of small communities as providing special opportunities of moral development. The other, closely connected with that, is that of using a shared reflection on Scripture as the main light shed on our motives, plans and actions. Our perception of that light leads us to recognize the presence of God in the moral experience of ourselves and of so many others, and so to the sense of wonder and thanks expressed in the Eucharist. In other words prayer is at the heart of any full kind of Christian morality.

4 The older approach saw Catholic life as largely separate from that of others—even that of other Christians. The Vatican Council recognized that the Church has learnt much about human values from the insights and examples of the other Christian churches, and of all men and women who are trying to live responsibly.

Christian Unity an Ecclesiastical Pipe-dream?

Should these developments be conducted by Catholics in partnership with other Christians? Many Catholics would say that some partnership is theoretically desirable but that in the foreseeable future it is unlikely. The situation is similar to that of the British soldiers in the First World War. Before they met German soldiers, it was easy to shoot at them. But when in a Christmas truce they were found to be peop.e with anxious families back home and ordinary human feelings, it was more difficult. Few Catholics have experienced a shared Christian life with Christians of other churches, apart from an occasional joint service. The members of other churches are 'them'. Their feelings and attitudes belong to a different world as unknown, very often, as that of the German soldiers. This robs unity between the churches of any felt motivation. Reports of their dwindling congregations make unity seem even less important. Is there, to be blunt, much good to be served by our trying to come together when we have more than enough to do already? And even if it would be particularly useful, isn't Christian unity an ecclesiastical pipe-dream? Have the churches' efforts at Christian unity amounted to any more than 'Christian Unity Week' and some esoteric gyrations by theologians? Some local initiatives have been laudable no doubt. But in general what is the good of trying to come together? What fruit would we be looking for?

The answer depends on your view of what a Catholic's vocation is. If we take the view that most of us grew up with, we see our vocation as 'being a good Catholic'. This meant practising the virtues that God and his Church require and hoping

96

that our good example, and the truth of our beliefs, would gain us heaven, and in God's good time be perceived by those outside the Church.

This was certainly a true and admirable ideal that led many to holiness. During the long period when the role of the Spirit in the Church was inadequately recognized by the Western Church, it was the best ideal available. But now that we recognize that the Church is the primary means by which the Spirit can be lovingly and creatively present in the world, we are coming to realise the truth of the Council's declaration that 'the pilgrim Church is missionary by her very nature.'[3] The Christian's vocation is to enable the people around him to see for themselves the possibilities of love and creativity that Christ offers all men and women, because they see these in what the Church and her members do.

A major obstacle to this at present is that a Church *whose purpose* it is to preach the brotherhood of mankind is largely uninterested in being a brotherhood. Instead it seems largely content with worshipping and working as indifferent neighbours rather than as concerned brothers. Suspicion, if not fear or disdain, seems often to be more powerful than love. And a Church that is constantly, and rightly, asking society to put people before blind adherence to institutions seems unwilling to practise this itself. The Church was founded to *say* creativity and love in a community that exists for the world. Its own internal relationships seem to belie that.

This is the problem. What solution can be found?

No Solution without Local Leadership

The general lines of a solution have already been indicated. The general feeling that Christian unity isn't made by theologians is obviously correct, and is frequently acknowledged as true and proper by theologians themselves. This kind of unity is *unity in living*. It emerges when people are inspired by a common love for Christ and one another to join together in Christ's work. They are responsive to the Spirit in the lives of

97

one another; in one another's service to those in need and efforts to lead loving and moral lives. It is impossible for them not to feel that they belong to the same community. Together with them they *are* the local church. As members of the same Spirit-led community, they must share one another's love, pray together, make decisions together, and give an account to the world of their common conviction that Christ is the way, the truth and the life. Only in this way can they really live a life 'directed by the Spirit'. Only in this way is true 'renewal' possible.

But how can this happen? Here two facts are important. First we will want it to happen only if we see the Christian's task as working with Christ. And the second is that our present structures make it extremely difficult in most circumstances for this to happen, even for those who want it to.

Someone has to help us get used to sharing and fostering our common inspirations and translate them into action. In virtually all urban parishes the priest can do this to a very limited degree. With his many other tasks he will have very little time available for such work or for learning enough of the theology of the other churches to help the members find a common language. The ministers of the other churches could at present fulfil only part of that role.

The Pope and many bishops are quite clear about the import-ance of the task. In June 1979 the Pope declared, 'One of my principal tasks [is] that of striving to bring about the unity of all who bear the name of Christian.' He called the present disunity a 'scandal [that] must be resolutely overcome', and in his November visit to Turkey he ran great risks in order to try to do that. He appreciates that that unity will be achieved, not primarily through conferences and statements, but 'as the result of cooperation among pastors on the local level, and collab-oration at all levels of the life of our churches.'[5] In England the Conference of Catholic Bishops cooperates extensively with the national bodies of the other churches. The will among senior Church leaders is there. But the structures that would enable that will to be implemented on any substantial scale simply don't exist.

Once again, then, an essential development in the Church is frustrated largely because we are attempting the logistically impossible. The deepest insights of the Council demand ten times as many leaders if they are to be put into practice. Our present unbiblical insistence on giving full powers of leadership only to clerics makes those insights more unrealizable every year as the clergy decline in numbers, increase in years, and lose, in many cases, their enthusiasm for a hopeless task.

Today's Special Opportunities

In the right circumstances, however, the task isn't hopeless at all. Ready to be used is an enormous improvement *in approach* that has been built up over the last few decades.

1 First, the Churches are **at least officially committed to unity** not (as is sometimes said) because their memberships are declining but because they realize that their disunity is a major obstacle to their representing Christ to the world: in short, as the Pope expressed it, it is 'an intolerable scandal'. We should not forget that this realization is relatively new. In 1928 Pope Pius XI condemned the ecumenical movement and forbade Catholics to have anything to do with it. In 1979 Pope John Paul II declares that it is 'one of my principal tasks'. This change has arisen from the reflection of all the churches on the fundamental nature and purpose of Christianity. It has been seen that our disunity 'openly contradicts the will of Christ, provides a stumbling block for the world, and inflicts damage on (our) proclaiming the Good News to every creature.'[6]

2 Second, we are becoming aware of the fact that **it isn't mainly differences in doctrine that keep us apart,** but 'barriers of nationality, race, class, general culture and, most particularly, slothful self-content and self-sufficiency'.[7] This was recognized 90 years ago by an Irish Catholic bishop. 'The existing diversity of opinions arises', he wrote, 'in most cases . . . from ignorance and misconceptions which ancient prejudice and ill-will produce and strengthen, but which could be removed.'[8] We forget that an essential condition of true discipleship of the God of the Hebrews has always been, from Abraham onwards, a willingness when necessary to relinquish even our most cherished cocoons. Yet all of us have seen in our own families the human reality that underlies this. Brotherhood is impossible unless you are willing to stand in your brother's shoes.

3 This second realization helps us to appreciate the force of the third and main one. This is that **we are fellow-members of the Church**. We share a common baptism and a common faith, which commit us to the same brotherhood and the same work. When they were formulating the Council's *Constitution on the Church*, the bishops rejected the draft proposed to them that stated that the Church of Christ of the Creed *is* the Catholic church. Instead they chose to declare that it *subsists in* the Catholic church because it also subsists—though a Catholic believes to a lesser degree—in the other churches, and even in the Catholic church the Church of Christ is not fully embodied.

Differences of Doctrine

The Council was not ignoring the fact that there are differences of doctrine, but it was indicating that the long-standing habit we have inherited of seeing these differences as primary is a caricature of one of the most magnificent of God's works. In God's eyes, we believe, all Christian churches embody Christ to the world and their members are our brothers.

This is not to deny the importance of doctrinal differences but to put them in perspective. Their importance arises from the fact that the Church cannot fulfil its function of embodying Christ unless, as a body, it conveys his Good News to the world. It is true that it will convey this more by what it does than by what it says. But what it does will be really credible only if it can, as a body, give an account of the perceptions which inspire its actions.

The fact that these perceptions give credibility to the Church's life only if they are seen as inspiring it reminds us of the obvious fact that my belief in, say, the incarnation may be a model of intellectual correctness, but if it doesn't refer to a truth that illumines my understanding and experience of human life it is of no current use to my life as a Christian. Doctrinal agreement that comes over as common solutions to ecclesiastical cross-word puzzles is of no religious interest.

But granted that our effectiveness depends on doctrinal agreement and that it must be of the right kind, we have then to ask how complete this agreement needs to be and how we can best attain it.

The Vatican Council gave valuable guidance with regard to the question of completeness. It drew attention to the fact that 'in Catholic teaching there exists an order or "hierarchy" of truths, since they vary in their relationship to the foundation of the Christian faith.'[9] The Church has always recognized that its teaching derives principally from an experience that had two stages: first its initial experience of Christ, transformed and Spirit-giving, from which the Church takes its origin; and then, second, the period when the Church had to work out a common understanding of this experience. Within this period it held the three ecumenical councils 'in which the East and West met together in the union of faith and love'. [10] Consequently the doctrines expressed there are fuller and more central expressions of the Christian faith than those expressed in later Councils.

Of course this is only to spell out the reasons for what most of us would consider obvious: that disbelief in, say, the doctrine of the assumption is of far less damage to doctrinal agreement than disbelief in what the Church is expressing through the doctrine of the incarnation. For these reasons Catholic theologians are even asking whether the Catholic church would be playing fast and loose with the will of Christ if it did not insist on acceptance of the last two Marian definitions as a condition of entry into a 'communion of faith'.[11]

To deny the importance of the 'secondary' teachings of any of the churches would be to deny the presence of the Spirit in the Church. But we have to remember that the Spirit's action in *all* aspects of the Church's life is incarnational: that it speaks through men and women. We have also to remember that no human formulation can adequately express the presence of God in our lives. An example would be the Catholic doctrine of transubstantiation. Catholics sometimes ask whether Church unity is really possible since the other churches deny this doctrine. They are rightly pointing to the fact that the Eucharist is central to Christian life and that a belief that Christ is really present there is essential to the Catholic understanding of it. But no Catholic is bound to believe that the Church's *formulation* of that belief is necessarily the best one. The Council acknowledged that 'the influence of events or of the times has led to deficiencies . . . even in the formulation of doctrine' and that this 'should be appropriately rectified'.[12] Another church's denial of transubstantiation isn't necessarily a rejection of the doctrine it seeks to express, but may be a denial of the adequacy of *that particular formulation*. Thus in 1978, after six years of patient work, the Lutherans (who assert consubstantiation) and the Catholics issued an agreed statement on the Eucharist which declared that they hold the same belief in the real presence of Christ in the Eucharist.[13]

We tend to think of these differences as just a tiresome burden, even if not as bars to eventual unity. When we do, we are forgetting what art or literature are always showing us: that great perceptions are so rich that they can be expressed in different ways. We are also forgetting that these perceptions are of value to us only in so far as they are, in some way, 'real' for us, and that the challenge of 'getting inside' the way that other Christians live and express their Christian beliefs can impel us to 'get inside' our own more adequately.

4 What has been mentioned so far is of no use without one other improvement in approach. This is the recognition that the Catholic church 'as a human and earthly institution always stands in need of reform.'[14] Although that need is an inevitable consequence of the Church's being Christ's incarnate presence in men and women, it received little official recognition before the Council. The defensive attitude adopted towards the Protestant churches at the Reformation had made that impossible.

102

But the Council acknowledged that Christ calls the Church 'to that continual reformation of which she always has need in so far as she is an institution of men here on earth.'[15]

Christian unity will take place when we see in one another's churches a sufficient fullness of Christian life for it to evoke our unreserved commitment. For that to happen, we must find adequately practised in the other churches the values that the tradition of our church has brought us to see as indispensable.

So a Catholic could not fully commit himself to the life in another church if he believed it had insufficient concern for preserving the authentic teaching of Christ, for example on the Eucharist; while a member of a Protestant church could not fully commit himself to the life in the Catholic church if he believed it thwarted the life of the Spirit in the Church by repressing theological inquiry or by preferring autocracy to community.

But official recognition of the necessity of reform and of the general lines it should take is of little avail until it is put into effect. There needs to be an atmosphere of community and of freedom and spontaneity in the Spirit in the way that Catholics live their faith both in the local church and in official leadership. This gives added urgency to solving the problems mentioned in the chapter on Christian leadership.

Christian Unity in Practice
What would happen if we were to apply these new understandings in order to 'live together as far as possible the common heritage of all Christians' and stop providing 'a stumbling block for the world'?

Presumably we would start (as the Pope seems to suggest) at the local level. Only in this way can a church as a body of people be involved. So each locality would, as far as its circumstances allowed, share a common meeting-place for worship and shared social activity. This, the neighbourhood would see, is the centre of the Christian Church, where brotherhood is so important that inconvenience is accepted, and risks are taken.

Each church would first train and then commission leaders to promote the various activities of the local church. One kind of leadership, if there were suitable candidates willing, would be understanding and explaining to other members the customs and beliefs of their own and other churches. This task would be made easier as and when members of the various churches joined each other in prayer, social action, worship and (though not yet fully) the Eucharist. The members would see for themselves that it isn't chiefly doctrine that divides us as they learnt to recognize in different and sometimes better formulations, doctrines they themselves hold. With the guidance of their leaders they would see for themselves the necessity for development and reform in their own church as they experienced the strengths of others.

Of course there would be the dangers that go with any launching into unknown waters. In places where there is insufficient leadership to help the members appreciate both their unity and their differences, such a launching would be wrong. The important thing is that this should be an avowed aim, even though at first it might not be possible to implement it widely. People would see arising over the country the kind of Church that they want to see, and that Cardinal Hume recently described. 'I look forward', he said, 'to a Church that is truly catholic, that is open to a rich diversity of traditions and cultures, and that is closed to nothing good.'[16] It would be the kind of Church that faces and progressively tackles, as brothers should, its important differences, but which recognizes (with the Pope) that 'unity—whether on the universal level or on the local level—does not mean uniformity or absorption of one group by another.'[17]

Some Pioneers

This vision is more than a deduction from the Council's theology or the wishes of some Church leaders. Some are already seeking to give it shape. On Whitsunday 1979 in a joint letter read out in all the churches of the Liverpool area, the leaders of the six major Churches called on their people to intensify their efforts for Church unity. They appealed for more joint action at every level, so that difficulties and differences might be overcome. And they invited people 'to engage in discussions on an interdenominational basis'.[18]

They were seeking to build on what had already been started in some areas. In one town (Southport) a large number of Church people had met the previous year in the centre of the town and had voted overwhelmingly to go ahead with a united Church mission in 1980. The churches there publish a joint newspaper 'to help to make us all a bit more aware of what is going on in the area; what needs to be done; and of the Christian hope in the doing of it.' The reason they are doing this is because, in their view, 'separatism is the very contradiction of the Gospel.'[19]

What Archbishop Worlock was seeking in Liverpool, Cardinal Hume had begun to do in Westminster. Seven months before the Merseyside joint letter, he and the other six Catholic bishops of Westminster met the Bishop of London with his five other Anglican bishops to pledge to work together more closely in future.[20]

Not all the initiative is from priests. In 1965 a group of students at Queen's University, Belfast, began to question the Northern Ireland way of life, and, inspired by various communities they had visited, they decided to set up one dedicated to breaking down the social, religious and political barriers of their country. There are now 600 people who belong in various ways to this community of Corrymeela (Hill of Harmony), and 6,000 visitors come annually, staying for varying lengths of time. Bookings are arranged so that both sides are always represented.[21]

The time is ripe; the will is quite extensively present; but until the Catholic church awakes to the role of the laity, and to the structures needed to give that scope, the evidence seems to suggest that the lives of ordinary Christians will benefit in general very little from all this promise.

8

AND NOW?

On 1 April 1977 there was a Mass in memory of Cardinal Döpfner. The sermon was preached by Cardinal Suenens. He reminded the congregation that Pope Paul, four years previously, had declared that the work of the Council would remain incomplete until we had applied to our understanding of Christ and the Church a renewed reflection on and reverence for the Holy Spirit.

From this reflection and understanding must come action. The first task, he said, was to create brotherhood among Christians. We must come to realize that we *are* the people of God and that *together* we share the great responsibility to the world that this brings.

The Cardinal reminded his listeners why this can be done only if we open ourselves to God's Spirit:

Without the Holy Spirit
God is far from us
Christ remains in the past
the Gospel is a dead letter
the Church is merely an organization
authority is simply domination
missionary activity is propaganda
worship a superstitious rite
and Christian everyday life a moral slavery.

So to be a Catholic today is to be responsible for sharing in the task of offering life and hope to the world. This, in spite of all the suffering and anxiety it had brought him, St Paul considered his 'treasure'.[1]

It may be helpful to conclude this book with some of the questions that we need to face as a community, with the help of the Holy Spirit, if the Church is going to carry out that task in today's world. They are listed here to correspond with the chapters that discuss them.

Chapter 1: The End of a Long Winter?
'Grant that from this Council abundant fruit may ripen; that the light and strength of the Gospel may be extended more and more in human society' (Pope John XXIII's prayer to the Holy Spirit for the success of the Vatican Council). What fruits of the Council do you find particularly significant?

Chapter 2: Invitation towards Summer
In what ways are you helped to appreciate your relationship with God by (1) The Bible; (2) Your relationships with other people? Do you believe that this should be a time of special hope and opportunity for the Church? If so, what has led you to this belief?

Chapter 3: Family Life
Do you agree that today a married Christian is in a better position to recognize that in his or her marriage is where he can particularly find God?

In what ways would you like the Church to give more help to us in recognizing God in our experience?

Chapter 4: The Church and Divorce

Have we sufficiently considered the real reasons why marriage, and particularly Christian marriage, *should* be permanent?

Is it true that the loving relationship in a marriage can become irretrievably dead? (Cf. Dr J. Dominian, *Marital Breakdown*, Penguin, 1968.)

If so, should the Church consider whether, in such a marriage, the couple might, in some circumstances, be free to divorce?

Should the local church, rather than the diocesan court of law, normally represent the Church in its responsibilities with regard to broken marriages?

What help should the local church offer to Catholics (1) To save them from the breakdown of their marriages; (2) To help those who are divorced?

Chapter 5: Prayer

Why do we need to pray? Must prayer be the basis of any genuinely Christian life? How in practice can it be that?

Do we still tend to link prayer too much with words? If so, how can we correct that?

What advantages do some people gain from praying in small groups?

Should the local church be trained to assume a much greater responsibility in the formation of its liturgy?

Within a parish, is it desirable that there should be, so far as possible, different kinds of weekly liturgy, for the benefit of different temperaments and even stages of faith? (Cf. further on this Joseph Gelineau, *Liturgy Today and Tomorrow*, Darton Longman and Todd, 1978.)

In what ways can the Bible help our prayer?

What consequences might that have on how we use the Bible in our public prayer?

Should we try to recover the threefold purpose of the Christian assemblies of the New Testament (see page 47)? If so, how could we, in today's circumstances, best do that?

Chapter 6: Christian Leadership

In the early Church there seem to have been several ministries basic to the Church's life: pastoral overseeing, prophecy, witness, teaching, theology, liturgical leadership and preaching. Because of circumstances that no longer obtain, the ministry of pastoral overseeing absorbed all the others. Is this absorption still desirable? If so, to what extent?

We must ensure that Christian life remains true to the experience of Jesus Christ. In today's circumstances, how can we best do this as a community?

Popes Paul VI and John Paul II have stressed their desire to share their government of the Church with their fellow bishops. What should be the result of this?

Even in the Vatican Council documents there are traces of the view that the people of God are simply clergy rather than the community that embodies Christ to the world served by Christ's ministers. Does the former view survive today? If so, what are the consequences, and what, if anything, should be done?

In what ways does your local church engage in conversation with your neighbourhood about its contemporary problems to offer 'the honest assistance of the Church in fostering that brotherhood of all men which corresponds to this destiny of theirs'?

'Many clearly did not consider that their parishes at present were communities: "Most of my friends do not feel part of our parish," commented a sixth-former—a feeling expressed by many others in all age groups' . . . Many people mentioned that London parishes in particular are too big and too anonymous.' (*Your Response*, Replies to Questions asked of the diocese by the Bishops of Westminster, 1977.) If you live, or know others who live, in a large town, is this also your or their experience? If so, how could this be cured?

Would you agree that the atmosphere in the Church has improved, say, over the last ten years? In what respects are further improvements particularly necessary? What should be our contribution?

In the meeting of European bishops in Rome in 1975, it was generally agreed that the Church's teaching 'demands dialogue with the community as a whole'. How could this be conducted? What differences do you think it might make? On what subjects do you think that it could be particularly fruitful?

What is your view of the function of primacy, as described in the 1978 Anglican-Roman Catholic Statement, quoted on page 73?

Can there be a local church, the primary reality of Church life, without a change in the role of diocesan bishops?

In practice, do we need the help of an extended programme like the one conducted by the diocese of Newark, so that enough people in our diocese have experience of what new structures can contribute to our lives as Christians and so that there are enough experienced leaders to maintain them?

Do you agree that today, in the Church, we particularly need pioneers? What contributions do you find religious orders making in this respect? What more would you like them to do, e.g. in your parish?

Does the Church at present sufficiently recognize the complementary relation, as equals, of men and women? If not, what areas of the Church's life have you found to be impoverished by that?

Chapter 7: Today's Catholic

How can we become more aware of the joy and responsibility of our vocation to 'walk in the light'?

What practical differences should that make to our family life, our attitude to our work, and our other relationships?

How should moral guidance be offered to mature, educated adults?

Is it true that the Church's understanding of morality is changing profoundly, particularly as we recover a more biblical understanding of God?

What is the role of the Church's official moral teaching?

Is it important that the Church's official moral teaching should be in an organic relationship with the reflection and experience of Christian people? If so, how could this be better achieved?

'What is distressing is, not that the Church should be under pressure to follow secular patterns, but that it should not be leading them.' (John Coventry S.J. in *One in Christ*, 1978, p. 92). Do you agree? If so, what should be done to correct this?

How important is the pursuit of Christian unity? What are the main obstacles (1) In your local church; (2) In the wider sphere? What should we do to help overcome them?

'I look forward to a Church that is truly catholic, that is open to a rich diversity of traditions and cultures, and that is closed to nothing good.' (Cardinal Hume, April 1978.) Is this an ideal we should be really working at in our local church?

To what extent are the four aspects of God's presence among us (described in Chapter 2) coming to be appreciated better in the Church's life? What significance do you attach to this?

111

NOTES

Chapter 1: THE END OF A LONG WINTER?
[1] *Roman Catholic Opinion: a Study of Roman Catholics in England and Wales in the 1970s*. Michael Hornsby-Smith and Raymond Lee (University of Surrey 1980), pp. 73 and 125.

Chapter 3: FAMILY LIFE
[1] Quoted in *The Catholic Church: the United States Experience*, J. Woodward ed. (New York, Paulist Press 1979), p. 117.
[2] Bishop Patrick A. Kalilombe, 'An Overall View on Building Christian Communities', in Woodward, op. cit., p. 124.
[3] *Roman Catholic Opinion*, op. cit., p. 65.
[4] Ibid., p. 73.
[5] Ibid., p. 125.
[6] Ibid., p. 73.
[7] Ibid., p. 126.

Chapter 4: THE CHURCH AND DIVORCE
[1] Cf. Dr J. Dominian, *An Outline of Contemporary Christian Marriage* (Liverpool Institute of Socio-Religious Studies 1976), p. 15.
[2] In U.S.A. in 1968 the average was 2–4 years.
[3] 'Less than 2 per cent of the more than six million divorced Catholics in U.S. have received annulments', Mgr Stephen Kelleher in *America*, 1978, p. 356.

[4] Theodore Davey, C.P., 'Help for the Divorced and Remarried?' *The Month*, 1978, p. 151.

[5] Joseph A. Fitzmeyer, S.J., 'The Matthean Divorce Texts', *Theological Studies*, 1976, p. 224.

Chapter 6: CHRISTIAN LEADERSHIP

[1] According to a research officer at the Irish Episcopal Commission for Research and Development, recorded by *The Tablet*, 3 March 1979, p. 219.

[2] The history of the ministry has been very fully presented in Bernard Cooke, *Ministry to Word and Sacraments*. Philadelphia, Fortress Press, 1976.

[3] As Pope Pius XII said in 1946 to the Cardinals: 'The laity don't merely belong to the Church; they are the Church.' Quoted by Ursula Schnell, *Das Verhältnis von Amt und Gemeinde im neueren Katholizismus* (Berlin, Walter de Gruyter, 1977), p. 109.

[4] J. A. Möhler (1796–1838)

[5] Karl Rahner '*Geist und Leben*', 1960, pp. 119–32.

[6] *Dogmatic Constitution on the Church* 2: 9 and 10

[7] Ibid. 2: 12

[8] *Decree on the Apostolate of the Laity* 5: 26.

[9] *Decree on the Ministry and Life of Priests* 7.

[10] *Decree on the Missionary Activity of the Church* 5: 21.

[11] *Joint Letter of the Hierarchies of Germany, Austria and Switzerland* (Trier, Paulinus-Verlag, 1970), p. 56 (my translation).

[12] *The Church in the Modern World* 3.

[13] Ibid. 41.

[14] Ibid. 3.

[15] Ibid. 41.

[16] *Your Response*, Westminster Diocese 1977, where only a small proportion of the replies showed an awareness of the missionary responsibility of the whole community (though this is not brought out in the printed version).

[17] This vital matter is excellently developed by M. Legaut, 'Pour entrevoir l'Eglise de demain', *Lumen Vitae*, 1972, pp. 9–40. (I am grateful

to Bishop B. C. Butler, O.S.B. for indicating to me this important article.)

[18] *Decree on the Bishops' Pastoral Office in the Church* 11

[19] Karl Rahner, 'Pastorale Dienste und Gemeindeleitung', in *Stimmen der Zeit*, 1978, pp. 733–43.

[20] *Decree on the Bishops' Pastoral Office in the Church* 3.

[21] Ibid. 9.

[22] A lecture given in 1969 and reprinted in *Theological Investigations*, vol. xii, p. 12.

[23] Gregory Baum, 'The *Magisterium* in a Changing Church', *Concilium* I.3 1967, pp. 39–40.

[24] Quoted from the report on the meeting by Professor Kevin McNamara (now Bishop of Kerry), who was one of the theologians invited to the meeting, from his article on 'The Role of the Bishop', *The Furrow*, 1975, pp. 711–20.

[25] In 1925 Rome insisted that he give up his teaching place in Paris and subscribe to the literal truth of Genesis. He could not do the latter. The Holy Office (now the Congregation for the Doctrine of the Faith) rejected the requests of his superiors that he be allowed to publish, even up to his death in 1955. Cf. *Teilhard: a Biography*, Mary Lukas and Ellen Lukas, London, Collins, 1977.

[26] *The Anglican-Roman Catholic Statement on Authority in the Church*, 1978, p. 21.

[27] 'The Episcopal Office', *Theological Investigations* vol. xiv, p. 199.

[28] Ibid. p. 200.

[29] Ibid. p. 196.

[30] The material is published by the Paulist Press, New York.

[31] *Consider Your Call*, Daniel Rees, O.S.B. et al. (S.P.C.K.), 1978. pp. 91–2.

[32] Bishop Patrick A. Kalilombe, art. cit., p. 126.

Chapter 7: TODAY'S CATHOLIC

[1] 1 Tim. 2:12 and 1 Cor. 14:34.

[2] The Pope's Address to the U.S.A. Bishops, 5 October 1979.

[3] *Decree on the Church's Missionary Activity* 1:2.

[4] Speaking on 17 January 1979, *The Tablet*, 27 January 1979, p. 90.

[5] June 1979, *The Tablet*, 14 July 1979, p. 687.

[6] *Decree on Ecumenism* 1.

[7] *Report on the Second World Conference on Faith and Order*, Edinburgh, 1937, p. 259. (Quoted in Michael Hurley, S.J., *Theology of Ecumenism* (Dublin, Mercier Press, 1969), p. 30.)

[8] W. J. Fitz-Patrick, *The Life . . . of Dr Doyle*, 1890, vol. i, p. 203. (Quoted by Michael Hurley, op. cit., p. 29.)

[9] *Decree on Ecumenism* 11.

[10] Vatican Council I DS 3065.

[11] Cf. J. M. R. Tillard, O.P., 'Towards a Common Profession of Faith', *The Ecumenical Review*, 1979, p. 57.

[12] *Decree on Ecumenism* 6.

[13] *The Tablet*, 23 September 1978, p. 927.

[14] Pope Paul VI, 21 September 1963. (Quoted in Michael Hurley, op. cit., p. 68.)

[15] *Decree on Ecumenism* 6.

[16] Speaking at the Chantilly Conference, April 1978.

[17] June 1979. *The Tablet*, 14 July 1979, p. 687.

[18] *The Tablet*, 9 June 1979, p. 565.

[19] From information kindly supplied by Mgr. L. Alston of Southport.

[20] *The Tablet*, 25 November 1978, p. 1154.

[21] *The Tablet*, 24 March 1979, p. 290.

Chapter 8: AND NOW?

[1] The piece on the Holy Spirit was quoted by Cardinal Suenens from an orthodox bishop. Cf. *Herderkorrespondenz*, 1977, p. 265 *et seq*.

FURTHER READING

Recommended books and tapes (an asterisk denotes a tape)

3 Family life

*Christian Marriage, David Konstant and Dr J. Marshall (Ealing Abbey)

*Family Problems, Dr J. Dominian and Q. de la Bedoyère (Ealing Abbey)

*Married life, Dr J. Dominian (Ealing Abbey)

4 The Church and Divorce

*Divorce, Dr J. Dominian, Kevin Kelly, Vincent Nichols, Rena Howard (Ealing Abbey)

Marital Breakdown, Dr J. Dominian, Penguin 1968

*Why marriages can go wrong, Dr J. Dominian (Ealing Abbey)

5 Prayer

*How can I pray? Alan Dale, Derek Lance and Sr Mary Peter Scanlan (Ealing Abbey)

Liturgy Today and Tomorrow, Joseph Gelineau. Darton Longman and Todd 1978.

6 Christian Leadership

Ministry to Word and Sacraments, Bernard Cooke, Fortress Press 1976

*The Priest in the Church, Bishop Butler and others (Ealing Abbey)

*Religious Life Today, ed. Damian Lundy (Ealing Abbey)

7 Today's Catholic

Principles for a Catholic Morality, Timothy O'Connell, Seabury Press 1978

The Theology of Ecumenism, Michael Hurley, S.J., Mercier Press 1969.

Practical Theology Series
Edited by Edmund Flood and John Coventry

Today's Catholic
Edmund Flood, O.S.B.
(Introductory Volume)

Faith in Jesus Christ
John Coventry, S.J.

The Church
David Morland, O.S.B.

God
David Morland, O.S.B.

Married Life
Vincent Nichols

Divorce Problems Today for Catholics
Kevin Kelly and Jack Dominian

Moral Decisions
Gerard Hughes, S.J.

Parish and Worship
Anthony Bullen, Brian Newns and others

Teaching the Faith
Gerard Rummery, F.S.C. and Damian Lundy, F.S.C.

Christian Leadership
Edmund Jones, O.S.B.

Is Ours a Just World?
Valentine Fitzgerald

The Role of Women in the Church
Oliver and Ianthe Pratt and Peter and Patricia Worden

118